SELLING AIR

SELLING AIR

How to Jump-Start Your Career in Radio Sales

Bob Diamond
with Jay Frost

iUniverse, Inc.
New York Lincoln Shanghai

Selling Air

How to Jump-Start Your Career in Radio Sales

iUniverse books may be ordered through booksellers or by contacting:

iUniverse
2021 Pine Lake Road, Suite 100
Lincoln, NE 68512
www.iuniverse.com
1-800-Authors (1-800-288-4677)

Because of the dynamic nature of the Internet, any Web addresses or links contained in this book may have changed since publication and may no longer be valid.

The information, ideas, and suggestions in this book are not intended to render professional advice. Before following any suggestions contained in this book, you should consult your personal accountant or other financial advisor. Neither the author nor the publisher shall be liable or responsible for any loss or damage allegedly arising as a consequence of your use or application of any information or suggestions in this book.

ISBN: 978-0-595-47773-9 (pbk)
ISBN: 978-0-595-60164-6 (ebk)

Printed in the United States of America

CONTENTS

Acknowledgments

First and foremost, I have a deep debt of gratitude to Ann Haigis Banash and Maggie Haigis for seeing something in me that I didn't perceive and offering me a position as a sports director with no training at all. Their affirmation and continued support created an environment in which I could flourish. Also:

To Jay Frost, the co-author of this book and frequent golf partner.

To Jay Fidanza, M.J. Fowler, and Bill Wiles who've put up with me for many of these years as well as all of the "Ole WHAI crew".

To Phil D., a true "radio guy," who introduced a high level of professionalism to our sales organization and was instrumental in my personal success.

To Will Stanley who gave me "an offer I couldn't refuse" when things were a bit anxious and dark, and taught me a great deal about innovative radio and selling quality rather than numbers.

To all of my current professional colleagues in radio who put up with my crazy energy and remind me daily that I always have more to learn.

To Deb MacLean who always encouraged me to "stretch" myself and convinced me that I could be successful in business.

To my sister, Cheryl, who helped me through some really tough times.

To my son, Chris, who keeps me "young" and helps me be a good role model.

To my partner, Karen, who gave me the space and time to complete this project.

And lastly to my Mom, who would be so proud of me because no one cherished the written word more than she did: reading the entire *New York Times* Sunday edition with a magnifying glass, well into her eighties. Mom … this book is really for *you*.

BD

Preface

How would you like a job that, on a single day, allows you to:

- Generate enough business to pay all of your household bills for an entire year

- Work out for an hour at a health club (where the membership dues are paid for by your employer)

- Treat a favorite client to a nice lunch (again, paid for by your employer)

- Create and record an imaginative, award-winning commercial

- Attend a board meeting of a high-visibility nonprofit agency (where many of your peers are respected members of the community).

… and maybe have time at the end of the day for a few holes of golf?
Sounds great, doesn't it?

Well, with the right combination of talent, motivation, and hard work, plus a good measure of raw courage—as well as a little luck— radio sales can bring you days like this … even in a so-called "small market," such as rural western Massachusetts, where I live and work.

Success like this won't come right away, for sure. In fact, it may take five years or more to get to the point where you can enjoy a day like the one I just described (and you can be darn sure that even after *ten* years, there's no way that every day will be like that).

But when you *do* succeed in radio sales, the profession offers significant independence, financial rewards, and the satisfaction that comes from helping others in many ways. For example, thanks in part to my connection with a local radio station, I have devoted considerable time and effort as a volunteer, fundraiser, and board member in several charitable organizations. In fact, these efforts, rather than detracting from my sales career, have enriched it by allowing me to develop a vast network of friends, colleagues, and clients in my community.

I'm sure you've heard the saying, "The more you give, the more you get." This has certainly been true in my radio sales career. I've put in countless hours of focused, dedicated time and the rewards have been huge.

As you read this book, it's up to you to determine if this kind of life—and lifestyle—can work for you. If you have the temperament, motivation, skills, and patience required, I can guarantee that you will enjoy a wonderful life in radio sales.

About me

Generally, it's not a good idea for sales professionals to talk too much about themselves, but everyone who knows me is quite aware that I like to do just that—it's one of my quirks. And I do want to provide you with an understanding of why I think I am qualified to write this book.

For more than 20 years I have been the top sales producer for both a small privately owned radio station as well as for corporate-owned stations and a broadcast network operated by a publicly traded company. Although I graduated with a degree in counseling and human relations from the University of Massachusetts and practiced social work for 15 years, I have always believed that sales was—and is—my true calling.

My major responsibilities in the broadcast world have been to generate large amounts of revenue through sales and promotion, and to serve as a community liaison on behalf of the stations I work for. Because of my success, I was even awarded a small share of the ownership of one radio station and received a payout when the station was sold. (Ownership options are less common nowadays, but top-performing sales executives are rewarded with shares of stock at some companies.)

I currently work for a publicly traded company as a director of sales for four stations in western Massachusetts. I have major sales responsibilities for these stations with the opportunities to sell airtime on nine other stations owned by this company throughout western New England.

About you

Enough about me.

What about you?

Do you think you have what it takes to be successful in radio sales?

I've already told you about the "dream" day where you can close several thousands of dollars worth of business in the morning and play nine holes of golf in the late afternoon.

But what about this …

Have you heard about the 16-hour days? About spending three hours under a tent during the pouring rain at the grand opening of a children's petting zoo, or out in the open in oppressive heat at an all-day rock concert? Then there is always the client who insists, against your advice, on hosting a live broadcast with no real "draw"—and when no one shows up *you* get blamed! Or the times when a client wants to be on the air Monday morning and shows up at the station at 4:55 on Friday afternoon and expects you to spend the next three hours producing ads?

I have encountered all of these situations in my career. And there's more …

Have you heard about the resistance you'll typically encounter on a daily basis? About the business owners who refuse to speak with you, don't want to hear your message, toss your literature in the wastebasket, and tell you how lousy your station is?

Are you aware of how cutthroat the competition can be? How a client can give you $5,000 worth of business one month and, for no logical reason, hand it to a weaker competitive station for the rest of the year?

You'll run into all of these issues in radio sales, which means that you must possess a number of essential character traits to ensure your success. For example, you must be:

- *Goal-oriented*—You must meet (and preferably exceed) very specific sales goals. (This is not that big a deal. Individuals who set and work toward goals in any career are usually more successful than those who do not.)

- *Organized*—This means that you must be able to plan out every month, week, and day, sometimes down to the hour.

- *Resilient*—You will encounter resistance more often than in almost any other profession, and you must be able to bounce back quickly in order to capture the next piece of business.

- *Optimistic*—This is an ideal career for those who view life with a "can-do" attitude, because that's exactly what you need on order to succeed.

- *Assertive*—You very often must leave your comfort zone to close the deal on a piece of business. If you don't, you can be certain that a competitive representative will, and you may be shut out of an account forever.

- *Outgoing*—You are *always* meeting new people in radio sales … business owners, receptionists, employees, listeners, colleagues in your own company, and competitive sales representatives (not just in radio, but in television and newspaper sales as well). It's up to *you* to take the initiative and generate goodwill for yourself and your company.

If this sounds like you, then you are reading the perfect book to help prepare you for a career in radio sales.

About this book

This book features nine chapters designed to provide useful information about a career in radio sales. It is designed for anyone considering a career in radio sales and for sales professionals who have been newly hired by radio broadcast organizations.

Here are brief previews of the chapters:

Chapter 1: Good Air summarizes the advantages and rewards that come with a successful career in broadcast sales.

Chapter 2: Bad Air (Just So You Know) takes an honest look at a few of the reasons why some people *don't* consider broadcast sales as the ideal career.

Chapter 3: How to Land Your First Job in Radio Sales outlines the typical job search and hiring processes and provides tips on how to land your first job in broadcast sales.

Chapter 4: Getting Started provides an overview of the training you will complete as a newly-hired representative, as well as advice on how to shorten your learning curve.

Chapter 5: Basic Skills and Concepts covers basic skills and behaviors that are essential for communicating and establishing lasting relationships with your customers.

Chapter 6:.General Strategies and Tactics coaches you on some useful business approaches that will help you and your customers achieve important business objectives.

Chapter 7: A Day of "Selling Air" takes you along on a typical radio sales day, with client visits, production of radio spots, lunch with a customer, and so on.

Chapter 8: The Business of Radio, provides brief but valuable background information about the core business aspects of radio advertising.

Chapter 9: Top 10 Tips for a Career in Radio Sales concludes the book with the top ten techniques that have worked for me during my twenty-year-plus career in radio sales.

The book concludes with an appendix that features three brief but instructive anecdotes from my career, sample forms and documents, and a glossary of selected terms associated with professional radio sales.

Bob Diamond
So. Deerfield, Massachusetts
November 2007

Introduction

When I was a teenager, my sights were squarely set on a lucrative, high-profile career in the NBA.

No, not the National Broadcasters Association. The National *Basketball* Association.

This is true. My dream of a hoop career was no idle fantasy.

So how did I wind up selling air time for small-town radio stations?

Let's take a brief look at how it happened.

As a kid, I played basketball almost every day from the moment I could hold onto the ball with two hands. Right from the start, I demonstrated a pretty fair jump shot, and over time start I developed excellent "court vision," as they say on ESPN. Later, I was good enough to be a freshman walk-on at New York University. Back then, NYU had a pretty fair Division I program, and during that first year I got some serious playing time, including a few starts.

Regrettably, my hoops career was derailed by a fondness for rich foods combined with poor practice habits. I failed to stay on the squad the following year, and that was that.

Without hoops, my compass needle started spinning. I dropped out of school, and I had no clue as to what I wanted to be when I grew up.

One thing for sure, I had no interest in any kind of a sales career. I was a child of the sixties, definitely into the alternative lifestyles, and the thought of peddling merchandise to make a living was thoroughly distasteful. I longed for something fulfilling, an altruistic line of work that would allow me, Bob Diamond, to save the world.

Idealism is a great attribute ... but I needed to eat, and my favored diet at the time was hardly "alternative." Look at any photo of me circa 1970 and you'll see that I was not too much into tofu and sprouts. More like three Big Macs, a double order of fries, and a couple of chocolate shakes. I literally had to work to eat (and eat big!), so I went out and got—guess what—a *sales* job!

At that point, I was able to rationalize my way into it. Most sales jobs did not require a college degree, I was (and still am) a good talker, and I was actually recruited by a few companies because I scored high on their "sales aptitude" exams.

I spent my rookie year with Uniroyal Home and Auto in upstate New York, and I discovered right away that I was a candidate for Player of the Year. I can still remember how couples came into the store looking for those all-season radials advertised at $99.99 for a set of four or whatever it was. Oh, I sold them the tires all right, but I also made certain that they didn't leave the store without a new TV, a microwave, a refrigerator, a washer or dryer, or whatever else it was that I convinced them they had a need for.

It was fun and I was pretty good at it, but my idealistic side kept reminding me that I was supposed to be "saving the world," and I wasn't measuring up. I finally concluded that I could accomplish my objective one small step at a time in the field of social work. So I enrolled in a degree program and decided to specialize in helping adolescents and their families.

It wasn't long before some colleagues and I founded a halfway house for troubled teens, launching what I thought would be a career in a "helping" profession. At the time, there was no way I could have known that that the core interpersonal skills of empathy, listening, and assertiveness that I developed would be essential in my later career in sales.

Over time I made the transition from working with teens to counseling alcohol and drug addicts and their families at a publicly funded substance abuse clinic. At this point, I was certain I would obtain a masters degree and devote the rest of my life to helping those less fortunate than myself.

But just then, as happens with so many of us, a chance occurrence triggered a major life change. I had taken up tennis and one of my regular playing partners was the husband of a woman who co-owned the local radio station (back then, the town had just one station).

The two sisters who owned the station had seen me on the local public access television station hosting a show on alcohol and drugs, and they thought that I would do well as a morning sports announcer. The truth is that they wanted a sports announcer who could double-up on part-time sales, but they did not communicate this to me at the time. Think about it: There are thousands of people out there sending out resumes and auditioning for radio jobs every day, and here I was being courted for a position when I had no inclination whatsoever toward a radio career. I took the job, and thus began my career in radio.

As with any newly launched career, the early months were not easy. In fact, after about a year of 60-hour work weeks—plus turning in at one o'clock in the morning and rising at five in order to write my sports stories—I was already close to the burnout point.

Along the way, I figured out that if I was going to make it big as a sports announcer, I would need to move around and work my way from small market to mid market to big market if I was going to earn a decent living and a reasonable level of recognition. I was already into my middle thirties, and I really was not up to competing with all the newly minted communication graduates entering the field with far more training and energy. Plus, I was very much attached to my home turf in western Massachusetts, which offered a stress-free lifestyle and unlimited opportunities for enjoying the outdoors.

While assessing my options, I noticed that sales staff at the station appeared to work far fewer hours than I did. I also figured out that they made a lot more money than I did. This annoyed me, but I also determined that the problem was not with the station but with me. I had it within my power to change my income, and I could do it right there at the very same place of employment. So I took on the dual tasks of morning sports announcer *and* part-time sales specialist.

I wish I could honestly say that I made a seamless transition to sales, but that was not the case. The first issue that I had to deal with was the fact that I could not be an effective salesperson while continuing with sports announcing, which was really my first love. As it turned out, events unfolded incrementally. Recognizing my desire to earn more money, station management added an administrative job, which included answering phones and doing work on the station logs and billing.

Back then there were no computers, fax machines, internet, or e-mail, so most of you cannot imagine the drudgery of turning out reams of paperwork on an old-fashioned electric typewriter. You had to cover up every error with white-out, then re-key the text over the dried-out mess—or else type the entire document all over again.

Suffice it to say I was not happy in this role, but I was earning more money … incrementally, as I said earlier. Plus, I always believe that every turn in life delivers new opportunities—*if* you are willing to take advantage of them. In retrospect, I can now see that all those hours of drudgery enabled me to learn all the ins and outs of the *business* side of the radio broadcast industry. Without this foundation, I doubt that I would have achieved so much so quickly when I eventually entered fulltime sales.

When a fulltime sales position opened, I made the move. At this point I knew a *lot* about radio—but, beyond tires and appliances, I knew next to nothing about selling air. Yes, *air*, because that is the product that a broadcast sales professional peddles, and hence the title of this book. To be more precise, a radio salesperson sells *time* on the *air* that allows an advertiser to reach thousands of listeners with a message. There's a lot more involved, and I'll get into that later in the book.

The best thing I had going for me at the time was the fact that my station was the only one in a community of 15,000, so there was absolutely no direct local competition. We were really the only show in town. Things were looking pretty good.

Just as I was settling in, I was recruited for a sales position in the home improvements business. The job had absolutely no appeal for me, except for the money, which was substantially more than I was making at the radio station.

As the interview neared its end, I told the business owner that I had decided to stay put at the radio station. He responded by offering me another $5,000 (his initial offer was already $5,000 more than I was making at the station, and that's back when an extra $5,000 was serious money).

At that point, an inner voice kicked and said, "This is a great opportunity. If I was 25, I would take this job in a second. But I'm 37 and I need to have at least the illusion that I am sort of my own boss, and I need *flexibility* in my work day."

The choice to stay in radio was one of the best decisions I have ever made. Over the next couple of years my career took off. My intuitive selling skills just kept on getting better as I opened all kinds of new accounts and soon became the sales leader at the station.

Today, more than twenty years later, I am still going strong. Although the small-market radio industry has changed dramatically because of deregulation and consolidation, I have adapted and thrived.

The money is great. The flexibility is exceptional (something I have had to earn over time), and the action never ends. It's a *great* career, and one that I want to tell you a lot more about.

The funny thing is, ask any successful radio sales representative how he or she got started in the business and the story will usually be a variation on the same theme. Like me, most sales representatives sort of stumble into it, or latch onto a job when they've run out of other options.

But that's not you. You're reading this book because you are actively interested in selling air.

So let's get started ...

CHAPTER 1

▼

GOOD AIR

So … you're considering radio sales as a possible career. Successful sale professionals must think positively. With that in mind, I'll begin by presenting all of the advantages that this wonderful career provides.

You are your own boss

Okay, you'll always have a sales manager and you'll always be required to attend sales meetings (every day, at some broadcast companies). Plus, you'll always deal with budgets, quotas, projections, paperwork, and mandatory company functions (sometimes fun, sometimes not). In fact, as the broadcast industry becomes more centralized, formal business structure now comes with the turf.

Still, at most companies, after your initial training period you are pretty much on your own and responsible for creating a daily schedule that works for you. There are actually times when it will seem like you are an independent contractor. As you will quickly learn, it is up to you to prioritize your sales calls and manage your own time in a way that will allow you to meet your sales objectives. If you are productive early in your career and demonstrate that you can independently achieve your sales numbers, money will naturally come your way, as well as increased flexibility in how you run your workday.

For me, this type of flexibility is worth its weight in gold. In my career, I quickly discovered that if I had a medical appointment, a school conference or athletic event for my son, a friend who needed a ride—or if I simply needed an hour or two to slow down and smell the coffee—then I have generally always had the freedom to do so. For most of my career this has been the best "perk" associated with the job.

Sure, every boss you'll ever have wants you to be working all the time, and any sloughing off of your responsibilities is counterproductive to your success. However, if you achieve your individual sales goals and help the organization enhance its bottom line, then my take is that you have *earned* the right to a degree of elasticity in how you manage your time.

Believe me, one of the true joys of this career for me has been the sense of individual achievement and freedom that I enjoy almost every day. Hopefully, the new, large corporations now dominating the broadcast world will understand that this is one of the reasons why their top performers continue to produce.

Your compensation is performance-based

Think for a moment of the different ways in which professional basketball players and professional golfers are compensated. The NBA star, perhaps fresh out of high school, gets a few million to sign on with a team, a few million more each year in an escalating contract, and probably a sneaker deal on top of that ... and he hasn't played a minute!

Now think of the typical professional golfer. Every tournament paycheck a golfer receives is based on his or her performance on that particular weekend–nothing else. If the top pros run into bad luck in the opening rounds, they miss the weekend cut and return home with zilch. The men and women who win the big tournaments *earn* those six-figure paychecks handed out on Sunday afternoons. It takes thousands of hours on the practice range and years of competing on the tour.

I'm sure you've already figured out at this point, that just as it is in professional golf, in radio sales you have to *earn* virtually every penny that comes your way. Almost always, the broadcast salesperson's compensation is commission-based. If you don't make the sale, you don't get paid. It's that simple. Your employer may provide you with a base salary, but eventually all or part of that is an "advance" or "draw" that is deducted from your commissions.

Also, as with most careers, in radio sales you have to start at the bottom. If you're a beginner, you had better have a spouse with a decent income, be living with the folks, have a savings account or trust fund to draw from, or expect a spartan lifestyle for a few months. This is because, unless you are handed a few existing accounts, you have a lot of hard work to do to get up to speed.

Now for the good part: Broadcast sales professionals—those who work hard in the early going and hang in there for several years and develop strong relationships with their accounts—are rewarded handsomely. Even in small markets (which is really what most of this book is all about), a successful salesperson can generate $50,000 to $75,000 or more per year in annual income, which is not bad at all considering other career options in non-metropolitan areas. (If you do work in a metropolitan area or mid-market, where the work is a lot harder and the competition a lot tougher, successful, experienced sales professionals earn $100,000 and upwards.)

The bottom line message is this: If you can sell, you will succeed. Later, I will tell you how to make it happen

Attractive perks

Because broadcast sales representatives work behind the scenes for their organizations, they are most definitely not media "stars," but when you consider the perks that come with sales, you might start to think that you really don't need all the glory when you get all these goodies that go along with the job.

Very often, radio stations sponsor or co-sponsor special events in and around your communities. These include concerts, grand openings (retail stores, restaurants, movie premieres, etc.), and trade shows (home and garden, boats, skiing, travel, etc.). On many occasions, you must work at these events (and they require a lot of hard work), but you do get to attend free, and sometimes in a highly visible capacity. Many times I have "emceed" at these events. Plus, most of these events are fun, and there is nothing wrong in my book with having fun on the job.

Helping others

There are several ways a career in radio sales allows you to "give back" to your community. If you believe deeply in helping others out, as I do, then there are endless opportunities along these lines. I will talk more about this later, but (as I emphasize several times in this book), I strongly feel that the more you give in life, the more you get both professionally and personally.

First, you give to your clients by helping them enhance their business revenues through the medium of radio advertising. Many businesses in small market areas have no clue regarding marketing and advertising. They are experts at what they do, but they typically have no training in marketing and are sincerely interested in learning. If you are properly trained by your company, you can help your clients create effective multimedia marketing campaigns. Of course, usually—but not always—you want radio to be a part of the mix. I have had a few clients for whom, in certain situations, radio did not make the most sense, either in terms of target audience or return on investment, and I told them so. More often than not, the owners of these businesses returned to me when the time was right for a radio campaign. They remembered that I provided valuable advice without pushing my own product on them.

In any event, very often all it takes is one well-written radio ad combined with an effective broadcast schedule and you—the radio sales professional—are perceived by a client to be a valuable agent of change … and that client will keep coming back

There's more than just the business angle to the 'giving' thing, too. As a broadcast professional, you'll discover many ways to give back to the community at-large through the relationships you'll develop with local nonprofit organizations.

Largely thanks to my contacts through the radio business, I have been an integral player in my local YMCA, Big Brothers Big Sisters, chamber of commerce, community college, historical museum, animal shelter, and many other community organizations. This not only provides me with a tremendous sense of helping others, but it contributes to business success, too. Nonprofits, after all, have advertising budgets … plus many individuals who serve on boards or participate in fund-raisers are members of the local business community. The business contacts you make through community service are incredibly beneficial. It's win-win for everyone.

Career progression

Career advancement after a start in professional sales has proven to be a big benefit for thousands of people in the broadcast world. I firmly believe that if you learn how to sell "air" then you can successfully sell just about anything.

It's often said that it's hard to find good salespeople because all good salespeople have jobs! It's true. I have been a part of countless job searches for salespeople that have lured hundreds of applicants, and on many occasions we were unable to attract a single viable candidate, let alone a handful worth interviewing.

Keep in mind that selling an intangible such as radio "air" is more sophisticated than selling widgets or appliances or cars, so most sales veterans will tell you that if you succeed here, that you'll do well selling almost anywhere else. Thus, when you develop a strong resume in radio, your options are almost limitless. For many in the broadcast world (especially in small markets, where earnings may be limited), the move up to selling more tangible products is often a "no brainer."

Of course, if you want to stay in the radio business, you have a number of options available to you, including:

- Advancement to a larger market area, with corresponding opportunities for increased income

- A sales management position at the firm you are already with

- Starting your own marketing and advertising firm

Virtually, all of the successful general managers, vice presidents, and even CEOs I have met in the radio business have significant experience in sales.

Your benefit package

The recent consolidation of the US broadcast industry has its plusses and minuses, but one of the definite plusses is the improvement of employee benefit packages for fulltime staff. When I entered radio in the 1980s, benefits such as 401's, employee health insurance, and paid sick days generally did not exist.

Nowadays, thanks to the buying power of consolidated broadcast corporations, small-town radio employees typically enjoy benefits more in line with our colleagues in major metropolitan markets. If you catch on with the right organization, you may even enjoy extra bonuses and expense accounts, in addition to routine mileage reimbursement.

Part of a team

In a society that values individual success and riches, at most radio stations (or networks), you can share in the excitement of team success in ways that many of us experience in team sports. Good management promotes an effective teamwork environment that features common goals, mutual trust, and shared rewards.

So now you know about the many benefits you'll enjoy by promoting "air" for a local radio enterprise. Sounds like a very attractive career, doesn't it?

Let's take a closer look …

CHAPTER 2

▼

BAD AIR (JUST SO YOU KNOW)

Every career has some drawbacks, and radio sales is no exception. I feel obligated to acquaint you with some of the less-than-positive issues that accompany this career choice. Selling radio airtime poses some significant challenges for everyone who ever tries it. Some succeed and some don't. You work in a highly competitive—some would say cutthroat—environment. I don't want you to try radio selling only to become frustrated, disappointed, out of work, and upset at me for leading you on.

So let's take a closer look at some of the major challenges that all small market radio representatives encounter in their careers.

Long hours (at the start)

Many of you probably fantasize about the prototypical nine-to-five job and assume that radio sales will fall nicely into that comfort zone. Wrong. You're not even close! New hires are always lowest on the totem pole, so expect to attend weekend live-remotes, evening civic and business functions, early morning chamber of commerce breakfasts, and so on. Keep in mind, however, that this is definitely an investment in your future success, and it's all necessary for the development of a productive network, which ultimately is the key to your success.

You can probably figure on putting in at least 55 hours per week at the start. At least that's about what I averaged in my early days back in the 1980s. And that was for a standalone, small-market AM-FM outlet. Today, the newly-hired sales representative is more likely to be a part of a regional broadcast network, so the demands on your time may be even more severe.

Low pay (to start)

You won't get rich quickly. In small regional markets like the one I work in, expect a starting base pay of between $15,000 and $20,000; in mid-markets—and even some small markets—you can expect more, probably in the $25,000 to $35,000 range.

Of course, most radio sales compensation is commission-based. This means that the salary is usually considered a "draw" until you start generating a similar amount in commissions. From that point on, you will typically operate on a commission-only basis. Here's an example. If you start with a salary of $17,500 (about $1,430 a month), your first $17,500 in commissions are applied against that amount—you receive no direct commissions; anything above $17,500 in commissions is yours to keep.

Some organizations keep the salary-plus-commissions arrangement as your compensation throughout your tenure with the company. This means that, using the example above, the $17,500 is "base" pay, and all commissions are awarded on top of that.

Commissions, incidentally, usually run at about 15% of the value of the time you sell. Thus, if you contract for $1,000 worth of airtime, $150 of that is yours to keep ... before taxes, of course.

Traditionally, the highest paid salespeople are compensated primarily on commission since they've built up a tremendous base of business and do better financially than they would with a salary-plus-commission structure. These individuals usually have an expense account that includes mileage, cell phone, and other work-related expenses. These packages vary among companies (be sure to have your expense policy spelled out in writing before you begin selling).

As you can see, when you start out, you might want to consider living awhile longer with Mom and Dad, or have a spouse or partner who can help cover your expenses. Usually, because of the time demands, another job is out of the question.

But don't worry … if you are good at what you do, life gets better. First-year total earnings in a small market can reach the $30,000 range—or even higher—and incremental earnings can get you to $40,000 and up by year three. Six-figure annual earnings are not unusual for seasoned veterans … but it takes a long time and a lot of hard work to get there.

Break-in period

I mentioned early that the art of selling an intangible—airtime—is significantly more difficult than selling widgets or washing machines. Selling air is even tougher than selling more "tangible" advertising, such as newspaper ad space. At least you can see a newspaper ad, and clip it out for saving if it has a coupon or an important time and date on it. Fortunately, in today's world, you can e-mail a client an ad via MP3 pretty quickly or bring them a CD to hear. Thus, you can, in effect, "show" your customers what they are purchasing!

My experience and observations of others in this business suggest that—assuming no media experience and excellent selling instincts—it takes a minimum of two years before a new representative can really hit his or her stride in radio sales. Although this is an excellent career for people, like me, who thrive on "instant gratification," you must be patient.

When I started out, I had excellent sales instincts, worked well with numbers (a requirement in this industry), and even had prior sales experience in retail appliances. Yet two years into the job, I still felt like a fish out of water, and I remained dependent upon my manager for advice and mentoring.

Intense competition

In this business, you must aggressively compete every day for your clients' scarce advertising dollars. Competitors typically include at least a half-dozen other radio stations, two or three newspapers, television, billboards, direct mail, and the internet. And, if that is not enough, today's satellite radio further complicates the picture. So expect a few battles out there. Plus, local schools, charities, and service organizations are all pressing advertisers to help sponsor events and buy space in yearbooks, programs, and so on.

With all of this going on, it's not at all unusual for a potential client to look upon you as just another sales rep trying to make a fast buck. As a colleague of mine said, "Every morning in this business, you have to get out of bed, don the helmet, and get ready for battle!"

Rejection

Radio sales is far from the ideal profession for sensitive souls who have a difficult time dealing with rejection. In fact, fear of rejection is a major issue with tens of thousands of people considering sales positions in *any* field. Here's the reality: You are very likely to fail to close a sale on at least eight out of every ten sales calls that you make.

The secret to success is not to let the eight "failures" get you down. Focus on the two "yes's" and grow your business from there. The "no's" are rarely personal, and they are not really failures on your part. Clients have other strategies, They may have used up their advertising dollars, or they may not be well educated on the value of radio sales (an issue I'll talk about later).

The bottom line is that you *must* be able to shrug off the rejections, learn from them, and zero in on the wins because those clients are likely to represent the key growth area of your business if you service them well.

Here's a story from my collection … One Monday morning, I walked into an account that I had been calling on for many years. The advertising buyer—not the owner—started my week with this lovely greeting. "What are you doing here? Just leave and never, ever come here to see me about radio advertising again!"

I lamely muttered a few words about my scheduled appointment, but I was so stunned that I basically staggered backwards out the door. Despite my generally optimistic nature and my resilience in the face of rejection, I was very upset, especially because I considered this individual to be a personal friend outside of our work environments.

Guess what? Twenty-four hours later the same guy called essentially demanding that I come in and see him right away because he wanted to get some ads on the air that very day! This single interaction taught me a lot about not taking things personally. This particular client apparently had some "personal stuff" going in his life that had absolutely nothing to do with Bob Diamond or any radio station. The two of us never mentioned the incident, and his business continued to be an excellent account for many years.

Pressure to perform

Pressure to do a stellar job is endemic to any career, but especially in sales. In the radio world, a sales career in the 2000's can be especially challenging. Pressure to perform has increased in recent years as most stations in the country are now components of large, publicly traded media companies. This means that boards of directors. CEOs, middle managers, and regional and local sales managers are under intense pressure to deliver profits and satisfy stockholders. Thus, the sales representatives who work the trenches operate under very close scrutiny in their efforts to achieve projected goals, even if they may be somewhat unrealistic.

When I entered the business, I operated relatively independently as sort of a "freelancer" who drew my paycheck from a single organization. Those days are gone forever, and fortunately I have been able to adapt. But it has not always been easy. Face it: If you are committed to working how, when, and where you want to, you have to be able to compromise.

This does not change the fact that you still can manage your own "business within the business." There are simply fewer options for flexibility and self-definition than there were in the 1990s.

Minimal training

When you launch a sales career with a major corporation, you are very likely to complete a formal sales training program that can last anywhere from a couple of weeks to six months.

Not so in radio. Virtually all of the training is informal. You'll probably have a mentor (usually the sales manager or a more experienced colleague). You'll also be handed a carton-load of cassette tapes, CDs, and DVDs that you'll be expected to complete on your own time. You'll also attend sales meetings with the staff and may even attend a generic sales training seminar.

The bottom line, however, is that you will be expected to learn as you go. Stations like to run "lean and mean" these days, and they tend not to invest resources in training their sales representatives. Sales mentors are often distracted with their own responsibilities, and all too often the idea is to throw the new representative to the wolves and see what happens.

Sad to say, management at many organizations seem to think that the "survival of the fittest" works best in this environment. I'm not one of those believers. Self-motivated, instinctively skilled salespeople will succeed despite a lack of training, but life could be a lot easier for stations if they devoted more time and money to their rookie representatives.

People, people everywhere

Virtually all top sales professionals are "people pleasers," and in radio sales you are interacting with all types of personalities all day long. It never ends. This suggests that radio sales is not the best career choice for those who prefer solitude.

And when I say all types of personalities, that's exactly the case. Frankly, I am not at all fond of about 15% of my clients. On the other hand, I thoroughly enjoy working with the other 85% who are fun, caring, interesting, hard-working, and sincere, Dealing with the bad apples is really a small price to pay.

Think about it carefully. Do you need "alone time" during the day? In radio sales, unless you work in a broad geography where you spend a lot of time in your car, you're almost always around people.

One more point in this area ... You must be able to interact effectively with individuals who often operate under stress. Many of your colleagues at the station ... general managers, sales managers, traffic specialists (individuals who accept and schedule the ads), other sales personnel, and even the friendly receptionist will sometimes lay into you, often for no other reason than that they are having a bad day. Of course, this is true in every workplace, but in the fast-paced world of radio where every precious second counts, the intensity level can be pretty severe from time to time.

*   *   *   *

Are you still with me?

Good. A lot of people try radio sales and give up because they are frustrated by one or more of the items covered in this chapter. I don't want this to happen to you. If you're serious about selling air, take some time to think about how these issues apply.

For now, let's find out how to land that all-important first job in radio sales.

CHAPTER 3

▼

HOW TO LAND YOUR FIRST JOB IN RADIO SALES

You'll recall from the introduction that I sort of stumbled into my career in radio sales. Selling air was definitely not a career goal when I enrolled in college, but after trying out a few other employment options, then landing a sportscaster job, I successfully made the transition.

Think about this for a minute: How many high school and college students do you know who have said to you, "I'm planning for a career in radio sales?"

Not many.

That's just the way it is in this field. Selling radio time is typically far removed from most everyone's radar screen—at least until an individual needs a job and has exhausted several other options. Like me, many radio sales professionals have launched their careers by accident, very often after exploring other options, or shifting over from other responsibilities at broadcast companies. (Many on-air personalities have made the shift from the broadcast booth to the sales department for a variety of reasons—for example, more money or, because they are good communicators, they seek an opportunity to interact with more people on a daily basis.)

One more point before we talk about your job search: There are no prerequisites for this job other than the ability to communicate with people, a professional manner (in demeanor and appearance), and the desire to succeed.

A college or associate's degree (especially with some business and marketing courses in the mix) might be helpful in securing an interview, but it is certainly not essential. Among the salespeople I have known, I would say that about two-thirds to three-quarters have a four-year degree. As I said above, you do not need the degree to succeed; you just need the motivation.

Age and gender don't matter either. You can launch a successful radio sales career at virtually any point in your working life, and many of the top performers in the field are women. Because sales representatives are paid on performance, there is no "glass ceiling." (Still, age and gender discrimination are illegal, but it can happen in individual broadcast companies just as it can in any other industry. I would caution you to be on the lookout for possible bias in either of these areas.)

Okay, so how do you get started?

Start online

Finding where to work in radio sales is certainly a lot easier today than when I got started. This is mainly due to the many options offered by the Internet.

Chances are, you'll want to work in or near your current location, so go to the websites of the local stations in your area. Check to see if they have a "Jobs" or "Employment" tab on the home page, and learn what's available. If you find a posted job opening, chances are you can respond right away online with an e-mail cover letter and your resume.

You can also take the shotgun approach and use your favorite search engine to locate "radio sales jobs." I used Google to do just that, and the response showed more than *24 million* possible listings.

Few of these sites are likely to list positions in your community, but you never know. Several sites post openings from all over the country, and you can sign up to receive e-mail notices of openings that meet your specification. At the very least, you'll want to at least browse and research many of the listings for no other reason to learn more about your options in radio sales and the types of qualifications that stations and networks look for.

A good place to start on the internet is *CareerPage: The Source for Radio and Television Broadcast Jobs.* This is a free service of the National Alliance of State Broadcasters Associations, and the site is accessed at www.careerpage.org. I just checked out the site and found about thirty sales positions posted during the past month. Many of them did not require experience—just a "need to succeed," which I stressed earlier.

Next, try any of the major national broadcast company sites. These include Clear Channel, Infinity, Citadel, Saga, and others. Again, many of the sites will have a clickable "Employment" tab that lists jobs and explains application procedures.

After that, try some of the comprehensive job search sites, such as monster.com, run a search for "radio sales" or "radio account executive," and see what comes up.

(Incidentally, if you know how to access the Internet, this suggests that you already have basic computer skills, which are absolutely necessary in today's radio sales environment.)

How to land that first job in radio

There are as many ways in the door as there are doors.

If you are in college, get involved with your college radio station.

If you are out of college and looking for your first job, check with your college's career center.

If you are looking for a career change, think about those aspects of your background that give you skills in a particular area. Teachers, for instance, often make excellent salespeople, because selling involves teaching clients how advertising can help grow their businesses.

Some college and community radio stations enlist volunteers to host programs during school breaks and summer vacation, in order to keep the station in operation. This is a great way to learn your way around the radio broadcast environment. [Keep in mind that many successful radio sales professionals, including yours truly, launched their careers behind the microphone.]

If you are willing to begin with an on-air position, volunteer for the less attractive time slots, just to get that proverbial foot in the door. Be willing to work the overnight, weekend and holiday shifts that no one else wants. (Recall that I was up at 5 a.m. every day to compile my sports broadcasts.)

Look into internships and training programs; many stations offer them. While an internship may not give you a paycheck, it provides hands-on experience and a resume entry.

Hang in there and be persistent (but not obnoxious). The maxim in sales is that it takes 30 "no's" to get one "yes."

Adapted from *CareerPage: The Source for Radio and Television Broadcast Jobs,* a free service of the National Alliance of State Broadcasters Associations, www.careerpage.org.

It's who you know …

Of course, very often the best entrée into any business position is a personal connection. You know the old saying, "It's who you know," and it often holds true in broadcasting. That's how I got my start. Over the years, I have met several people who I thought were "naturals' for radio sales. I pointed them in the right direction, put in a few good words with management, and several have gone on to enjoy success in field sales and sales management.

What particular traits suggested that these individuals were tailor-made for a radio sales career? Most important to me were their superior communication skills, especially their ability to connect with another person right away. They also demonstrated the motivation so critical for success and advancement in the radio business. They displayed creativity, too, especially their ability to conceptualize marketing and promotional opportunities. If you think you possess these characteristics and can secure a "sponsor" in your radio job search, you will have a huge head start on the competition.

The reality is that most of you reading this book probably don't have a friend or family member who is connected to the industry, so you'll have to search the Internet and help wanted ads.

How can you prepare?

So how can you prepare to take advantage of the first job opportunity that you spot? First, you can assess your own personality type. Many broadcast companies nowadays require sales applicants to complete a variety of written tests that may assess everything from personality traits to basic math skills.

Some of the larger companies have identified specific personality characteristics that they think are essential for success in radio sales, and many of these companies will not hire individuals who fail to meet these criteria. It certainly doesn't hurt to know in advance what some of these questions might look like, so it's probably worth your time to browse a few of the career/personality tests available online. Start by checking out the free test at www.livecareer.com

In terms of the math skills, I'm talking about very basic stuff here but you often need to perform some basic calculations in your head or on a scratch pad—percentages, multiplication of a dollar rate times a number of ads, and so on.

I've noted a few radio sales professionals who are woefully weak in the math department, but they are definitely a minority. I seem to be blessed with good intuitive skills when it comes to numbers. Not only can I perform rudimentary calculations very quickly, but I have easily committed almost all of my clients' phone numbers to memory, which is a real timesaver.

Are you "hungry"?

Let's return to the subject of motivation for a minute—because it is so critical to success in this business.

It will always depend on what a particular manager, company, station, or manager is looking for, but in today's marketplace I always hear the word "hungry." Managers want people who are "hungry" for money and success. There are plenty of "lifers" on radio sales staffs—these are successful sales reps who have a long list of established clients providing a steady revenue stream. These types of reps rarely need to pound the pavement to generate business.

That's not the type of individual today's sales managers need when they're looking for a new hire. Instead, managers are looking for individuals who need money and want to make lots of it. The ideal candidates are willing to spend the long hours required up front to learn the business and *relentlessly* grow their networks of clients while encouraging current clients to buy more air.

There are, of course, two sides to this issue. "Young and hungry" usually implies a willingness to work tons of hours while sacrificing personal time (many young people are not yet worried about spending time with family) What manager wouldn't want a dedicated, tireless, vibrant up-and-comer who'll devote 24 hours a day, 7 days a week to the organization?

But then consider the client's point of view. Certain clients prefer to do business with an experienced individual who demonstrates a certain degree of life experience, someone they can more easily relate to. The average 50- or 60-something business owner might have a tough time relating to a 22-year-old hip-hop sales rep a few months out of college … which is one reason (mentioned earlier) why age does not matter. Many sales managers will enthusiastically hire qualified representatives in their forties and fifties for the very reason that these individuals may be able to interact more effectively with established local businesses.

Regardless of your age or motivation, the drive to succeed is the one personality characteristic shared by every winning radio rep I have known. During your interview(s), you will need to impress your prospective employer with your drive, your willingness to be trained and to do things *their* way, and your enthusiasm to get out and comb the local area for every available lead and dollar.

Don't confuse "hungry" with "desperate." There is often a fine line that separates the two. Clients don't respond to reps who present themselves as desperate. This attitude translates into impatience—the stereotypical "pushy" representative. Instead, the ideal representative must be both driven and patient at the same time; and the first time to demonstrate this is during the interview process.

The interview

In small radio markets, the average applicant pool for a sales position typically averages at about 30 prospects. Most of these individual respond by e-mail with a cover letter and resume in response to newspaper ads, web postings, or local college bulletin boards.

Usually, if you are among the top five or so candidates, the sales manager or an administrative assistant will call you to schedule an interview. In some cases, the station may ask you to complete an on-line personality test before you show up, and you will receive instructions on how to do so. (You may complete the test at the station, in conjunction with your interview, discussed shortly.)

Dress "up" for the interview. The station may in fact have a liberal dress code, but you want to present yourself just as you would for the station's most important clients. (You'll find more on how to dress in Chapter 5.)

Your first interview is likely to be with the sales manager only, and here are a few of the questions you are likely to encounter:

- What attracted you most about this job?

- What is your impression of what this job entails?

- What achievements are you most proud of?

- What can you tell me about your prior employment experiences?

- What motivates you most in a working situation?

- How much do you know about our station (or network)?

After the formal interview, you may be asked to take an online personality test (if you have not completed this earlier), and you will be set up at a workstation. These tests try to measure performance tendencies and work attitudes in some of the following areas:

- Dominance (A reasonable level is desirable, but not too much.)

- Influence (Employers will look for a high score here.)

- Steadiness (A medium score is good. Managers want people who can think on their feet and are not too caught up in doing things just one way.)

- Compliance. (Managers want employees who play by the rules, yet they also like it when potential sales representatives demonstrate willingness to take risks in certain situations.)

Results are usually accessible instantly, and the sales manager make take the time to discuss results. The two of you may actually review the scores and personality summary produced by the software.

If the test results strongly suggest that you do not meet the requirements for a radio sales career, the interview may come to an end right there. There may be some additional discussion that provides a window of opportunity for you, but if that particular station relies heavily on test scores, the manager will very likely extend regrets and wish you better luck elsewhere.

If you survive to this point, the manager may proceed to a higher level of questioning where you may be asked:

- What skills and aptitudes do you think make you appropriate for the position?

- Given that eight or nine out of every ten sales calls result in a "No," how will you react to rejection?

- Are you willing to put in a lot of extra hours at the start?

- How involved are you in the local business community?

You will probably have the opportunity to ask some questions of your own about the station and the position. If you have not already been informed, you have every right to ask about compensation, benefits, expense accounts, employer expectations, performance reviews, and so on.

One manager I spoke with says that he tries to intimidate applicants by confronting them with some of the harsh realities that anyone new to the profession will encounter. Because you have read this book, you will already be familiar with these issues, so you should be ready and willing to deal with them.

If you're still in the running at this point and the general manager is available, he or she may be brought in to meet you and may ask you a few questions.

If all goes well, you will probably be asked to be on call for a second interview. If the station definitely wants you back, the manager will schedule an interview and you may receive an appropriate "homework" assignment. For example, you may be asked to prepare a mock presentation for a retail business or write a 30-second spot for a real or hypothetical business.

During the interim, it's a good idea to call the sales manager with a question or two about the assignment. This demonstrates that you are interested, assertive, and understand the concept of pursuing an objective—which is crucial in radio sales.

If you return for a second interview, you are probably one of just two or three finalists. Or you may get a call and receive a job offer, at which point you need to *ask* for a second interview to go over terms of employment, or at least ask about them on the phone.

If you are a beginner, you probably have very little leverage regarding pay levels. If you have previous sales experience, you may be able to negotiate slightly higher compensation, but in most situations you simply have to prove your worth through performance in the field.

For now, let's assume that you survived the hiring process (which can take up to three or four weeks). You were selected from thirty or forty applicants, agreed to your terms of employment, and are set to report for work on a certain date.

What should you expect during your first few weeks at your new job? The next chapter provides some clues.

CHAPTER 4

▼

GETTING STARTED

It's your first—or maybe second—day at work. You've completed all the tax forms, attested that you are not a wanted felon, selected your insurance coverage (if you're fortunate enough to have any), read the employee handbook (if there is one), and discovered the locations of the coffee bar, the refrigerator, and the rest rooms.

Now it's time to learn your way around the station, meet the people you'll work with, and get ready to sell some air.

Take the tour and meet your colleagues

While taking your tour, chances are you'll meet most of your team members at the station. Following are some general descriptions for jobs in the radio broadcast industry. It's important to note that each station is unique in its staff arrangements and job titles—no two stations are alike. The size of a station its market area usually dictate staff size and positions. At small-market stations, for example, a single individual may assume two or more of the job titles described below.

I've listed the following positions alphabetically (credit the National Alliance of State Broadcasters Associations and its *CareerPage* for jump-starting me in the development of these descriptions):

- **Account executive**. This would be you. In the real world, the official job title of almost every radio sales professional is "account executive," and that is what it will say on your business card. Account executives (or "AE's") sell advertising time and work closely with businesses (accounts) to help them market themselves to the station's listening audience.

- **Announcer**. Announcers are the radio station's "voice." They are usually the personalities with whom the public identifies. If the station is music-oriented, the announcers are the familiar disk jockeys, or DJs. Announcers introduce programs and music, play or read ads and public service announcements, and are often involved in live broadcasting events. If the station is all-news, all-talk, or all-sports, then the announcers' primary responsibilities will lie in those specialties.

- **Copywriter.** This *could* be you. Large stations may employ a staff member to write commercial and promotional copy for some of the station's clients (many clients provide their own ads) … but at most small-market stations, the sales staff is often responsible for writing copy for local advertisers who lack the resources to hire an ad agency or the skills to write copy on their own.

- **Engineer.** The station's engineer manages the technology that delivers the station's broadcasts to its service area. The engineer works to maintain broadcasting capabilities and provide quick solutions to problems that arise with the transmitter, tower, satellite receiver and related equipment. It is not unusual for the engineer to get called to the station in the wee hours of the morning to solve the problem when the station loses power. The engineer may also install and perform preventive maintenance on the station's control consoles, boards, recording equipment, microphones, and other station equipment and electronic systems

- **General manager.** This is the boss—the person responsible for the overall operation of a station. This position requires business knowledge, leadership ability and a technical understanding of how a station operates. At small-market stations, the general manager is often the business owner as well

- **Music director.** This person manages the station's music library and works with the program director in selecting new recordings to be played as they are submitted by record companies. At small and mid-size stations, the music director is usually a senior disk jockey.

- **News director**. The news director manages the news department, assigns stories to reporters on staff, monitors wire service newsclips, and identifies the important news issues within the community. In small markets, the news director usually travels with a recording device in hand and attends town meetings, political rallies, major fires and accidents, and other newsworthy events.

- **Production manager**. The production manager assigns announcers, schedules studio time, arranges recording sessions, produces commercials, and directs programs.

- **Promotion director**. This individual promotes the station's image, programs, and activities in the community. He or she works closely with the program director (below) to create on-air promotions. The promotion director also interacts with the sales staff to help secure new clients and retain current advertisers.

- **Program director**. This person is responsible for the entire on-air product. The program director manages the overall "sound and feel" of the station, with control over production, talent, work schedules, and program schedules, all to support the goals of the general manager and the sales manager.

- **Receptionist.** Receptionist duties vary according to the size of the station. In addition to answering the phone and greeting walk-in visitors, this person may also handle other administrative and support responsibilities outlined here in some of the other job descriptions.

- **Sales manager**. This individual hires and supervises the sales staff, reviews programming for the best sales opportunities, develops sales plans and goals, oversees billing, analyzes ratings, understands the station's market, and approves all sales promotion campaigns. Larger stations and broadcast networks have multiple levels of sales managers, including national, regional and local sales managers.

- **Sales assistant.** This position provides support to the sales staff by handling much of the paperwork, including drafting proposals, which allows the sales staff to focus on meeting with clients and developing business. Small-market stations often do not have the luxury of a sales assistant and account executives typically must generate and manage their own paperwork.

- **Sports director**. The sports director produces and delivers daily sports reports and often handles play-by-play coverage for local sporting events. Stations typically employ part-time "color" announcers to complement play-by-play personnel.

- **Traffic manager**. This individual collects commercials and programming information from other departments in order to prepare a minute-by-minute schedule for the broadcast day. The traffic person is the daily link between the sales department and programming department, keeping the sales staff up-to-date on commercial time availability.

Okay.... now that you have taken the tour and met the staff, it's time to learn your job responsibilities.

It's about time ...

Once you are shown to your office (which may be a standalone office or a cubicle in a large room shared with the rest of the sales staff), you'll figure out that one of the most important things you'll need is time to adapt to your new environment ... lots of it.

To ensure your success, you must know the station and the radio business inside out. During your first few weeks on the job, be ready to put in lots of time and effort to educate yourself. I recommend that you keep a notebook (or a file in your computer) and take lots of notes.

Some stations inundate their new hires with tons of training tapes, videos, books, CD-ROMs, and so on, many will require you to pass an exam based on the training materials. I never went through this process, but people whom I have talked with say as long as you put in the time, it's fairly easy to score 100. So don't sweat the training program. Just do as directed.

Computer literacy

Virtually every job today requires that the employee be competent with a computer, and radio sales is no different. Your skills on the computer will save much time and aggravation. At a minimum, you should possess good word processing skills. If you are able to use graphics programs to enhance your proposals and create e-mail promotions, so much the better. Your manager will definitely take note.

A lot of sales activities are supported by e-mail these days, so you need to quickly learn the station's e-mail program and learn how to send attachments and open them up on the receiving end.

Believe it or not, there are still a few "old-line" general managers and sales managers whose computer skills are slim to none, so it makes you "shine" if you're a computer whiz and can help make their lives easier.

In recent years, faxes, e-mail, internet access, cell phones, Palm Pilots, Blackberries, and so on have made the sales representative's job a lot easier and increased efficiency.

Acquire a mentor

Usually, a newly hired radio sales representative is teamed up with some type of mentor or trainer to help learn how things are done. Usually, this is your sales manager, but it might also be a senior sales representative on staff.

More and more, it seems, new representatives are asked to get out and pound the pavement with no on-the-job experience. I do not recommend this. You should be able to spend some time 'bird-dogging' with a high-producing account executive at the station. This means going out on sales calls, observing, listening, asking, and learning. If you are not assigned to a mentor, ask for one … someone who's a willing teacher and will take the time to answer all the questions you are likely to come up with. Remember, I was basically a pain in my manager's butt for a long time before I developed self-confidence in this business.

The first steps: CNAs and account lists

So what are the first steps necessary for learning the job?

Because the identification of customer needs is essential in *any* sales job, many stations require new representatives complete a *customer needs assessment,* or "CNA." Some employers may require you to complete twenty or thirty of these assignments with prospective clients.

CNA assignments require you to visit a prospective advertiser—either alone or with your mentor—and ask the business owner a series of questions about his or needs and goals regarding advertising. In some cases, your manager will provide you with a form to fill out during your initial customer interview. (If that doesn't happen, then it will be very helpful to create your own form that you can use with all of your prospective clients. I have included a sample form in the appendix.)

CNAs help you create foundations for effective sales representative/client relationships. You get to practice asking intelligent questions and you will learn a lot about the business and the individual that will help you develop an effective radio advertising proposal. This is a great way to work on your listening skills as well.

A few CNA visits may actually generate a sale on the spot, but this is really a time for you to learn about the client's business and potential advertising needs. Plus, clients tend to like it when you take the time to find out what makes their businesses tick rather than hearing you launch into a canned sales presentation.

For me, this type of hands-on learning was far superior to reading and test-taking.

At some stations, the sales manager will provide you with an account list, however small it might be. The accounts are usually local businesses, and many of them have not advertised on radio, or at least on your station. Some are new businesses; others have been around for a long time and have resisted radio advertising—perhaps the owners have a bias towards newspaper advertising (or another station).

Your account includes current and prospective advertisers that are yours and yours alone to call on. For most rookies, most of the accounts will be prospects because sales management will want you to demonstrate early on that you can develop and maintain new business. However, thoughtful sales managers will hand off at least one or two current advertisers to a newly hired representative. For one thing, having a loyal advertiser on hand from day one is a confidence booster; for another, you get to see what things are *supposed* to look like once you "own" an established account—a goal that you can visualize for all of the new accounts you'll be visiting.

Here's one thing to watch out for if you are replacing a representative who left the organization to take a job elsewhere. Clients sometimes use the previous representative's departure as a convenient excuse for canceling—or failing to renew—their current advertising package.

In these situations, it's essential for the new representative to move proactively, and quickly, in order to create a smooth transition that secures the relationship for the long term. During the changeover, ask your sales manager to accompany you on the first one or two calls. Better yet, if the previous representative is still with the company, have that person introduce you to your new client. Astute managers recognize the value of keeping existing accounts (it's a lot easier and less expensive than looking for new accounts); your manager won't want to lose any business, so he or she should be more than willing to help you out in this regard.

Become "known" in your community

Getting "known" is one of the biggest challenges in small-market radio. The more familiar you are among the local client base, the easier it will be for you to generate business for your company. The problem here is that you're always competing against well-known reps from competing broadcast companies, newspapers, and maybe television, too.

These seasoned sales pros can walk into a business cold and someone will usually have heard of them. Either that or competitive representatives will already have an established relationship with the account (whether the client is currently advertising or not); plus the other representatives already have confidence in their knowledge of the area, local demographics, and needs and trends among local businesses. They have anecdotes at the ready to engage their clients, and they are experts at "dropping" the names of clients and businesses with which clients are familiar.

There are two steps you can take to deal with this issue. If you want to get known in your community: (1) *Know* your community; and (2) make yourself *visible.*

Know your community. The sooner you become thoroughly familiar the area in which you sell, the sooner you will enjoy sales success. Remember, you're not selling a tangible item that people are begging for; you're selling a service about which your clients need to be educated. Your sales manager should be able to get you started, and your next stop should be the local chamber of commerce. (It may even help if you join a committee or event group at the chamber.)

One important concept is knowing your geography so that you can conveniently cluster your sales calls on a given day without wasting time and gas. Thus, its makes eminent sense to work a single neighborhood, town, or business district on Monday morning than it does to bounce around from place to place, spending a half-hour or more of your time between calls in your car. This is simply not productive. So get a local map of the area and plot out a call strategy. If you have a weak memory, mount your map on the office wall and use color-coded pushpins to identify your accounts.

Make yourself visible. You *must* have the ability to *engage your customers* in order to establish the rapport necessary for successfully completing a sales transaction, and one of the best ways to make this happen is to become a *joiner.* Start out by joining a civic group—the Lions Club, Rotary or Kiwanis; or volunteer for board or committee duties at non-profits, such as the local YMCA, United Way, hospital, or youth athletic groups. Right away, you will have a higher profile, plus you will meet many business owners and managers who are candidates for your account list (if they are not already on it).

This is not the only way to develop a presence in your community. Another productive activity that will help you achieve the same objective is to attend as many station functions as you possibly can during the early months of your tenure. Live remote broadcasts are a great way for you to learn how the station presents itself, to meet people, and to become comfortable making the "small talk" that is often important in a sales career.

After you participate in a few of these events, you will become relaxed and confident when meeting new people. Effective sales managers will encourage you to attend live broadcasts, as well as business breakfasts, trade shows, county fairs, and so on. The more you participate early on, the faster you will become an active and recognized functionary in the business fabric of your local community.

Learn the lingo

Like most professions, radio has its own "inside" language ... "Arbies," "morning drive," "PSA," "run of station," "30-second spot," "SFX," "cost per point," "Make-good" and so on ... you will need to learn it all, and the best time to do so is early on. So if you hear your boss or a DJ or the station engineer using terms you are unfamiliar with, just *ask.*

All of the members of the station staff want you to succeed, so they'll be more than happy to spend time explaining terminology and providing insights on station operations. Keep a notebook handy and wrote down key information. Then go home and study it. Odds are that you will one day have to articulate the concept to a client in a simple manner.

Make certain that you spend some extra time in the traffic, billing, and production departments. You need to understand how to place an advertising order, how the spots (ads) are placed in the station log, how ads are produced—and how to produce ads *yourself,* which is very common among sales personnel at smaller stations.

With computer programs such as Cool Edit Pro (a digital audio editing system), creating ads for your clients has never been easier. Getting a busy production manager to show you *how* to use Cool Edit Pro is another matter. At some stations, it may be best for you to sit in on a few sessions, take notes, and create a few practice ads until you get it right. Like most software programs, it's fairly intuitive so you'll definitely pick it up with repetition.

Of course, if your client needs a sophisticated commercial with lots of high tech sound effects, voiceovers, and so you will need the services of a production professional. I strongly recommend that you develop a cordial, cooperative working relationship with your station's production director. It will pay off handsomely for you many times over.

Create some 'spec' ads

After you've figured out what's going on, create a few "spec" ads. "Spec" is short for "speculative," meaning you have no clue if your ads will work or not. Write some up for 10, 15, 30, and 60 seconds so you develop a feel for timing. To get started, pick any local business—or a particular product from a business—and think about how you might create an ad that will cut through the clutter of all the advertising messages that bombard us every day. They keys are to make certain that people clearly understand the concept, benefit, or offer *and* will be moved to take the requested action.

Trust me, it's not easy, even for seasoned copywriters. Fortunately, you probably won't need first-rate copywriting skills right away because most stations provide their sales staffs with adequate copywriting support. Still, it certainly doesn't hurt to be able to write a quick, high-quality ad script when a client needs it in a hurry.

After writing a few ads, schedule a meeting with the production director to critique the ads and then to produce them with music, sound effects, multiple voices, and so on. This is a great way to get hands-on experience of the production process. Early in my career, I spent a lot more time with copywriting than I do now. For one thing, the station had a small staff, but I also had fewer accounts back then, so I had time to create ads. I consider myself very lucky in that regard. Knowing how to create an effective ad can be a very useful skill for the radio sales professional.

Practice with the mike

Here's another tip that you probably won't find anywhere else: Spend some time in front of a microphone. Do the voiceovers for the spec ads you created, and get a feel for talking into the mike. This is a great way to put yourself in your client's shoes, because many local business owners prefer to record their own ads (this is a very effective form of advertising ... just think of Colonel Sanders, "Dave" of Wendy's fame, Frank Perdue, David Oreck, and Lee Iacocca, to name just a few).

I'm lucky to have a decent, non-regionalized radio voice (remember, I got my start at the sports desk) and I still like to do ads for certain clients ... but I take care not to do ads when a client's business competes with other clients of mine. For example, even if I am close personal friend of a car dealer (e.g., for Ford or Chevrolet) but I also do business with another car dealer (e.g., Honda or Toyota), especially in the same region, I would not do the voiceover for my friend's radio ads. (There are some experts who say you should not even work with competing businesses, but in small markets it's hard to be a high-producer without having some of these conflicts.)

Bottom line: If you have a good voice, no noticeable accent, and feel comfortable behind the mike, go for it. "Starring" in your clients' ads can be an effective entrée into a solid relationship with the account, *plus* you gain some recognition in the community.

Organize your time

At the very beginning, your days will be organized for you. They will be filled with training programs, video tapes, reading manuals, watching others at work, and—if you're lucky—going out on sales calls with the station's high performers so that you can observe the different selling styles of successful sales professionals.

However, you will very rapidly reach the point at which you'll need to plan your own days, and let me emphasize: you *do* need a plan.

Because I have been at the job for so many years, I consider myself "old school" when it comes to mapping out the days ahead. I still use a traditional daily planner in which I schedule sales calls, other events, and "to do" items.

I generally transcribe my daily call lists and appointments from my planner onto a piece of paper in front of my computer. I keep the list with me in my car and refer to it throughout the day. For the past 20 years, this system has worked very nicely for me. I'll add other notes for shirt pocket if something is particularly important or I feel that I am at risk for forgetting an important item.

There are other methods of course. Many sales professional use electronic notepads; some use their computer to create daily printouts (using calendar systems or simply making checklists); others use a daily planner or a small notebook that fits a jacket pocket that they make entries in.

For me, my time is of the essence—as is my client's time—the so I need to be meticulous in following up on *everything*. I cannot afford to miss a bit, so I prepare my list, check it once, check it again, add and delete, and then *rewrite* it sometimes twice a day. It works for me, and I am rarely accused of missing details.

*   *   *   *

Okay, so you've spent your first few days as a radio station sales professional. You've met the staff, toured the departments, received your account list, and maybe even created a few practice spots.

It's time to hit the pavement and go out and sell.

How, exactly, will you develop skills in this area?

You'll find out in the next chapter.

CHAPTER 5

▼

BASIC SKILLS AND CONCEPTS

"Selling is no different than living. Like living, it's based on creating relationships. Master the art of selling, and you've mastered the art of relationships: indeed, you've mastered the art of living. Everyone lives by selling something. You can't quit. Anywhere you go you'll end up selling. So stay with it because this is your big chance to master life."

—Steve Chandler, *The Joy of Selling*

If there is one recurring lesson that I have learned throughout my sales career, it is this: When I sell with enthusiasm, I firmly believe that I can sell anything, whether it is persuading a client to contract for a month-long radio campaign, or convincing my golf partners that it is makes more sense to play at seven in the morning instead of noon.

Certainly, the ability to sell comes somewhat naturally to me, as it does with many successful sales professionals. Yet there are certain basic skills—whether you possess them now or need to acquire them—that must be mastered in order to continually develop and maintain a customer base.

In the context presented here, "basic" refers to the common-sense skills and behaviors that all sales professionals must demonstrate, regardless of the industry or product. In this chapter, I'll discuss these basic behaviors with a radio spin.

My intention here is to help lay a foundation for you. Hundreds of books have been written on the art of selling, including a few devoted exclusively to radio sales.

Positive attitude

I briefly mentioned in Chapter 1 that a positive attitude is a prerequisite for a career in sales. And here's a key point: you can *choose* to have a positive, upbeat attitude. Some sales representatives seem to naturally possess this attitude all the time, so they don't have to make the choice at all. But if you are like most people (myself included), and your mood can sometimes shift with the wind direction, *choose* the proper mood before you step out of your car into a customer's place of business.

This means that, regardless of what has happened up until the moment you greet your customer, you must remember to practice the following behaviors:

- Smile—a nice smile almost always wins friends and opens doors to businesses of all sizes and types.

- Remember first names of clients and their staff personnel, and ask how people are doing. Be sincere, listen to what they have to say, and remember their areas of interest so you will always have talking points when you return.

- Be courteous and respectful of what is going on around you. Your client's customers always come first. If the owner of a retail business needs to visit with a customer, accept the interruption with grace.

- If you tell a client that you will only require a few minutes of his or her time, stick to your promise.

- Maintain an "attitude of gratitude." Say thank you for every small sale, and for every small favor, including the time spent with the customer.

I am not suggesting that you put on phony airs or a plastic appearance. Above all, you must be yourself. The fact that you are in a sales position indicates that you have an upbeat personality, and that you are intelligent, articulate, and possess personal attributes that people like. Your own positive "uniqueness" is a great selling point so let it show.

Creating relationships with your customers (and their staff and employees) in radio sales is like building relationships with customers in any other line of selling. People buy the product, but they *also* buy the salesperson.

How many times have you gone to a retail store, fully intending to buy a certain product but not doing so because the salesperson was unfriendly, unavailable, or unhelpful?

On the other hand, how many times have you entered a store with the idea of "just looking" but ended up buying an item that really cost more than what you planned to pay simply because the salesperson smiled, identified your needs, matched you up with a product, and went out of his or her way to confirm that this was exactly what you wanted in the first place?

Both scenarios happen every day in the sales world. Try to make certain that the *latter* scenario plays out in *your* day-to-day selling.

Personal appearance

I'm not going to spend a lot of time on this. I have always taken great care in my physical appearance and selection of clothes, although I know a handful of successful representatives who seem to do okay without following this rule. The basic rule is this: You simply need to be well-dressed at all times when you are in the field.

Of course, "well-dressed" means different things to different people. If you're selling air for a country station, certain customers may be more than happy to see you in well-pressed jeans, an open shirt, and cowboy boots. If you're seeing someone who runs an alternative-life-style type of business (e.g., punk rock concerts, organic farm stand), then a three-piece suit may not be the smart choice. Of course, if your employer has a dress code, then take care to observe it at all times. If you have any doubts, check out what the other sales representatives wear—or ask your manager

On most days for me, the upper end of "business casual" works fine. This means dress shirt, pressed slacks, and usually, a necktie. For women, an appropriate dress or blouse-and-skirt (or slacks) probably works best.

Generally, I believe that radio sales representatives should dress for success and be impeccably groomed, preferably on the conservative side. On occasion I have observed representatives who have dressed *too* fashionably. This is to say that wearing a $900 Armani suite or a Rolex watch may not sit too well with local business owners and their employees. My philosophy is that your dress should simply say, "I'm a competent professional" and nothing more.

Basic communication skills

All successful sales representatives possess above average communication skills. These include listening, questioning, reflecting, dealing with objections, and so on.

Here are some of my personal suggestions in these issues:

Avoid "canned" presentations. In your training videos (if you view any), keep in mind that you are viewing actors reading from scripts. In the real world, in front of customers, you need to get beyond this "formal presentation" mode and focus on a conversational interaction.

In other words, don't simply march into a customer's place of business and launch into a carefully rehearsed script. Take the time to find out what customer's concerns are regarding advertising needs. In order to do this successfully, you must *ask good questions* and *be a good listener.* Let's examine both of these skills ...

Employ good questioning skills. You really can't sell anything to any-body—whether it's $500 worth of radio ads for a $50,000 luxury auto-mobile—without first identifying the customer's needs. And the only way to identify needs is by *asking* about them, then *listening* to what the customer says in response. (I'll cover listening in a moment.)

For example, if a retail customer is in a department store checking out refrigerators, a savvy salesperson will not simply launch into a presentation about the ice-maker, the water dispenser, and the energy-saving thermostat. The customer might not care about any of these features. Instead, the salesperson might ask: "How much space do you have in your kitchen?", "What color do you prefer?", "What price range are you interested in?", and so on. Questions like these help the salesperson deliver a presentation that matches a customer's precise requirements for a refrigerator.

It's the same way in radio. A good sales representative will ask specific questions that direct the conversation toward the advertiser's need to get the word out about his or her business. These needs could relate to almost anything, for example, a need to:

- Attract customers to a grand opening

- Announce the features and benefits of a new product line

- Promote a limited-time special offer or discount

- Maintain a particular image that has already been established

- Stay within a predetermined advertising budget

- Counter a competitor's current promotional campaign

    … and so on.

The point is, without getting answers to these questions, you might just as well deliver your presentation to a wall.

Virtually every selling skills program that you would pay big bucks for includes practice at questioning (or "probing") techniques, and each program seems to have its own spin on methods and terminology.

I won't get into specific methods here. My point is, during every sales call, always ask a few questions to identify customer needs and preference. The responses provide you with prompts that will help complete a successful call by effectively matching ads to customers' needs in line with what the customer wants to spend.

Be a good listener. I just mentioned this above, and this may very well be the most important skill a representative can have in his or her arsenal. Yet, it is surprising how many sales professionals (and how many of us in general) are poor listeners. Time and time again in selling skills workshops, trainers stage introductory listening exercises designed to test listening skills, and invariably, a fairly high percentage of participants fail.

You don't have to take sales training programs to practice good listening. You can work on this skill in everyday life when interacting with family, friends, store clerks, and fellow employees.

One good way to sharpen listening skills is to practice the related skill of paraphrasing. For example, in a sales situation, you might reflect on what a customer has just said by saying something like, "Steve, if I understand you correctly, you are most interested in building store traffic by promoting lawn and garden products at this time of year. Is that correct?"

Reflecting helps you confirm that you understand what the customer said and provides you with a starting point to position an effective radio campaign.

Other communication skills include such basics as maintaining eye contact, using sales aids as focal points for discussion, pausing for effect after making a key benefit statement, and acknowledging a customer's concerns and objections regarding your product.

Building rapport

Sometimes, advertisers on your station will become personal friends. This does not happen very often, nor should it even be a goal with every customer. Your professional goal is to encourage every customer you call on to advertise with your station or network.

My point is, when you become friends with a customer, you have succeeded at developing a high level of rapport. You'll discover many customers with whom you can talk comfortably about almost any subject, and where the informal banter flows easily.

Rapport occurs at many levels. You can, over time, establish rapport even with gruff, impatient, hard-to-see customers. With these individuals, you'll generally maintain a strictly professional relationship, which is fine.

In fact, with experience you will discover that the entire personality and psychological components of selling are very important. Many of today's advanced-level selling skills programs address this issue by training you to match your own personality type to the special personality of each customer.

You really don't need to go to that level of detail. Over time, you will develop a sort of "sixth sense" regarding the appropriate level of rapport to develop with each individual customer.

Create a goal for every call

One way in which some representatives fall down on the job is that they fail to set a goal for *every* sales call. It's one thing to have weekly, monthly, quarterly, and annual goals set by your manager. Some representatives just make calls on customers with no objective other than to simply get some face time and hope that things work out for the best. That is not enough.

Before you enter a customer's place of business, it's important to have a very specific goal in mind. Examples might include:

- Complete a customer profile or client needs assessment (CNA) (see page 24)

- Close the deal for a customer commitment to launch (or renew) an ad campaign.

- Collect information required for a new campaign

- Secure approval for a newly produced commercial

- Ask the customer to recommend your station to another business

Goals can be big or small. It doesn't matter, as long as you continue to advance the customer toward becoming a first-time (and then a continuing) advertiser on you station or network. Sometimes, securing new business will occur on the first call. In other cases, it will take weeks, months, or (if you are patient) even years. If you create goals along the way, it will be easier for you to track your own progress with every account and prospective account.

The skills and behaviors I have just outlined represent the plain-vanilla basics. The following chapter takes you to the next level by examining some of the more common strategies and tactics that broadcast sales professionals must be familiar with.

CHAPTER 6

▼

GENERAL STRATEGIES AND TACTICS

In the previous chapter, you learned about some of the basic skills you must possess in order to succeed as a professional salesperson. This chapter follows with some of the basic strategies and tactics that have worked for me and the stations I have worked for.

Just so you understand (because you'll hear the terms often): *Strategies* are the general plans and approaches you will take to help your clients achieve their goals. *Tactics* are the specific steps you take to implement the strategies. An example of a strategy might be to create traffic for a grand opening of a new retail store. An appropriate tactic in this case might be a radio ad campaign that features "saturation" 60-second spots during the week leading up to the grand opening event.

Cold calls: Yes or no?

A "cold call" occurs when a salesperson walks into a prospective customer's business off the street with no scheduled appointment. You simply hope that your prospect will give you some time, and if he or she does so, you go from there. This cold call is clearly less sophisticated than scheduled calls, and you must be able to think on your feet. It is typically the most difficult way to make a sale, but hopefully your least common mode of operation.

Although in many industries, the cold call is considered bad etiquette, there are still opportunities in the broadcast world for spontaneous walk-in calls. Some clients will insist upon appointments arranged in advance (always respect their wishes), but there are always a few who actually enjoy a brief respite from their daily routines. As you get to know your clients, make certain that you know their preferences. Don't do cold calls where they are not welcomed.

Cold calls can be highly intimidating when you start out, especially when you have your sights set on a first-time advertiser. However, when you think about it, you really have nothing to lose by trying, and these calls become easy as you develop experience and confidence. Early on, it's not a bad idea to observe your manager or mentor rep on a few cold calls so that you see how the process works.

Here's an example of when a cold call might be appropriate: Let's assume that you are driving down the local commercial strip and you spot a sign proclaiming the opening of a new business. First, call your sales manager on your cell phone and ask if anyone on staff has already made a connection. If you can't reach your sales manager, stop by the business anyway—the prospect will advise you if there has been contact.

Clearly, as soon as possible, you want to establish who the decision-maker is regarding advertising. Most of the time, especially with new businesses, this will be the owner or manager. In these situations, you usually have a short window of time to 'connect" with that person and establish a relationship.

I always try to connect on a personal level, finding out where they're from, how they got into the business and what their business is all about. I also try to make them aware that I have an understanding about the business world and that am an ally who can help them achieve their business objectives, as opposed to some fast-talking sales rep trying to win commissions for myself.

There is such a thing as the "planned" cold call—planned in the sense that you already suspect that the business is a good candidate for radio advertising and it is relatively easy to develop an "opener." These situations can occur when:

- You note companies that advertise in newspapers or local cable TV, but not on radio

- Your sales manager provides you with the name of a promising prospect

- A prospect calls in requesting information about placing ads (a signal that the advertiser probably wants to be on the air right away—so have a rough proposal ready!)

- You hear a spot on another station and you think that the business should be advertising on *your* station

Regarding the last point, *always* monitor other stations while driving around town or at home. You already know that the businesses that advertise recognize the value of radio advertising, but they may not understand that your station may actually represent a better buy because of programming type, demographic, cost, added-value services, and so on. This is where you need to *differentiate* your station from the competition—always focusing on the unique and positive attributes of your station and avoiding negative references to others., Also, generally with a company that already uses radio, you'll spend little or no time educating them about the benefits of radio. They already "get it"!

Newspaper bias?

With new businesses I try to find out early on if the owner is planning to advertise immediately or is in the process of figuring out how to effectively promote the enterprise. All too often I discover that they have already contacted the local newspaper! For some reason, local business people often think that newspaper should be their first choice for successful advertising even though countless highly successful companies do no newspaper advertising at all.

If you discover that an advertiser has already contracted with the newspaper, never look at this as a negative. For the savvy sales representative, this is really a great opportunity because your initial interaction will provide clues as to whether or not you will ultimately be successful with this potential client.

The first step is to stay positive. *Never* belittle the competition and talk about the weaknesses of print media. Similarly, avoid attacking the characters and motivations of newspaper reps (I count the local newspaper representatives among my good friends). The Golden Rule applies—you certainly do not want them badmouthing you or your station. (Of course if the new advertiser bombards you with statistics provided by the newspaper industry showing newspaper's strengths and radio's weaknesses, you might want to have an info sheet that shows the reverse. In fact, newspaper circulation has decreased markedly over the past several years while radio audiences have remained fairly stable ... and I have the numbers to prove it.)

Instead, focus on the many benefits of radio advertising (we'll get to them later) and the excitement and intensity that radio brings to its audience. At this point, you want the business to *add* radio to its advertising budget to complement the investment in newspaper.

Your short-term objective is for your station or network to be a least a part of their opening advertising budget. For example, if you are making a first-time call on a new business and you learn that the business is already committed to the newspaper–either with grand opening announcements or special-offer coupons—you might say something like:

> *Mary, newspaper advertising is a good choice. But my experience suggests that you build even more traffic for your store by combining newspaper ads with radio 'chasers.' For example, your radio ads might say something like, "Don't miss our two-for-one coupon in Friday's Daily Clarion!" This way, you can capture new customers who don't read the paper or, if they do, might not notice the ad.*

Keep in mind that life can be tough for small businesses when they start out. It's very difficult for these operations to establish a meaningful advertising budget with an effective media mix because the owners often have little feel for what to expect in terms of business volume, and hence revenue flow.

Spreadsheets and projections are great tools, but that's all they are. It takes weeks or even months to determine if forecasts are realistic. (I experienced this myself as part-owner of two restaurants and several other small businesses.) You can dream all you want about the riches that will come your way, but the public has a mind of its own. It definitely takes time and perseverance—and a lot of satisfied customers—to ensure the success of a new enterprise.

Grand Opening!

This brings me to the "Holy Grail" for every new business: the proverbial *Grand Opening!* It's no surprise that every owner of a new business wants to get the word out and generate a rush of new customers on the very day that the doors open for the first time. For every start-up entrepreneur, the universal fantasy is of a great celebration with hordes of customers lining up to be among the first to purchase the new products and services.

Let's examine the consumer's perspective. First of all, Mother Nature can determine the relative success of the event. Here in the Northeast for example, driving snowstorms or heavy rains are guaranteed to keep crowds down, regardless of whatever free samples, souvenirs, and discounts are part of the draw.

But let's say the weather is great. It is much more common for a retailer to be unprepared for the business launch—and if first impressions are negative, the general public will not likely forget their experience. Consumers expect superior service, favorable prices, sizable portions (for restaurants), sufficient stocks on featured items, and so on.

The reality is that most customers tell a *lot* of people if they have a bad experience but only a few pass the word if the experience is positive. With this in mind, my advice to retailers has always been to have *two* "openings." The first is a low-key, or "soft," opening which allows management to determine if systems, service, staff, and merchandise match customers' needs. Then later, when it is confirmed that everything is in place, a widely advertised grand opening is more appropriate. My observations are that over and over again, local business owners who take this route seem to generate more positive results. (Chain retailers and restaurants are a different story. They usually have the systems and staff—including nationwide resources—in place to open with a bang right off the bat.)

The first radio ad campaign

Okay, so let's assume that the new business is ready to develop its initial radio ad campaign *today*. How do you, as a radio sales professional, utilize your skills as a "consultant" and create what's best for your new client?

Here's a general rule of thumb to use as a starting point: The most productive radio advertising generally requires from 21 to 30 ads per week during "prime" listening times. Broadly speaking, this is from 6 a.m. to 10 p.m., Monday through Friday.

Peak times within that framework are the "drive" times—the hours when millions of listeners across the country represent a "captive" audience while commuting to and from work, taking the kids to school, etc.

Morning drive time (traditionally 6 a.m. to 10 a.m., but in most markets now 5:30 a.m. to 10 a.m.) refers to the period when consumers wake up, drink the coffee, primp and preen, and head for work or school. Afternoon drive time (3 p.m. to 7 p.m.) includes the afternoon and early evening hours when listeners travel homeward after their busy days. Drive times are the periods when the number of listeners is highest, and this is when radio stations and networks charge the highest advertising rates.

Roy Williams, the author of *The Wizard of Ads* and *Secret Formulas of the Wizard of Ads,* recommends as many ads as possible (called "saturation" advertising) that works backward from the day (or night) of a big sales event—as far as the advertiser can realistically afford.

What about the other times of day? Many stations grant huge discounts when advertisers purchase the overnight hours to complement your prime time advertising. For the beginner or novice representative, this is when an experienced mentor helps. For example, if you have a solid relationship with your sales manager, there's no shame at all in calling him or her right from the client site. If that is not appropriate, then get all the information you can from the customer (budget, campaign theme, date/time of event, etc.) and promise to return with a plan that meets the client's objectives. Then meet with your manager at the station, create a plan that works, and either hand-carry or e-mail it to the client.

Hand-carrying is better because face time with a client usually result in more—and bigger—sales than phone or e-mail contacts. (This is not to take away from the fact that you absolutely need to develop high-level phone-selling skills; and it helps to be able to create persuasive e-mails messages, too. Speaking of which, always try to start emails with a greeting, not just information. People are much more receptive when you've taken a moment to be polite.)

It is not unusual to make a first-time call (or even to receive an unsolicited advertising request) to a new business and generate orders on the spot. It happens. But if life in this profession were so easy, there would be no need to develop skills as a radio sales professional, and I wouldn't have written this book!

Adding value

What's great about radio is that in many situations you can offer your client "value added" advertising in form of special promotions. If, for example, your client is a sporting goods store, check with your sales manager and program director to see if they are willing to offer some sort of giveaway prior to the opening. A good idea might be to have an on-air sports trivia quiz where winners receive $25 gift certificates to the new store—and maybe a Grand Prize winner gets two tickets to a major league sporting event. or perhaps the retailer is willing to provide free T-shirts or ball caps with the store name and logo. The possibilities are limited only by your creativity.

Your program director or sales manager will probably base planning on the size of the package purchased by the advertiser—the bigger the package, the bigger the promotion. Together, you will work together to determine how much exposure the client will receive in terms of name mentions and "liners." (Liners are short "imaging" sentences or phrases that the DJ includes during an intro of a recording or during a break between songs and ads. Often, if the client's "buy" is significant, the station will mention the business name almost every hour leading up to the grand opening.)

For many businesses—especially at grand openings—there is an obvious opportunity tie-in for a live broadcast (or "remote") at the site of the event. Live broadcasts can be dynamite for the advertiser, or they can be disasters if they are not properly planned and managed. I will talk more about live remotes in Chapter 7.

(Incidentally, one of radio's greatest strengths is the fact that a station can respond immediately to a customer's needs and get an ad on the air in a very short time, which of course newspaper can't do. There are many times when a client has called and I have written quick commercials, and the ads have been on the air within an hour. Now *that's* added value! Getting right back to the client with a plan—or even an ad—can score major points with the customer. Of course don't rush to the point where the product is of poor quality. Make certain that both the scheduling and the commercial itself are well thought out and reasonably priced.)

The CNA and other ways to prepare

Recall that in Chapter 4 I introduced the idea of completing Customer Needs Assessments (CNAs) as a great way to get to know your customers. CNAs not only help you learn more about a current or prospective advertiser, they also appreciate you more when you express interest in their issues and challenges. As noted earlier, many companies will require you to complete a series of CNAs during your training period before you are allowed to sell.

Here's a hint: *Before* you visit a place of business to talk advertising, go to the customer's site beforehand, and visit their website, if they have one. This will provide you with clues on products, services, and the company's business style. When you show up in your role as a sales professional, the customer will be impressed that you took the time to be prepared.

Here's another idea. Before you visit the customer, check out the Radio Advertising Bureau (RAB) website at www.rab.com (or the site of your state's broadcast association). These sites have searchable links (your station will have a pass code) that provide you with all kinds of sales tips plus background information on issues and trends in virtually every submarket you can imagine.

For example, if you are planning to call on an appliance store, the RAB site provides you with articles on buyers' preferences during certain times of year, gender preferences when making buying decisions, price points of certain demographic groups—*plus* (this is very important) the average annual advertising expense for retailers in that segment.

As suggested earlier, some business owners may not have advertising budget and won't know what the standard is for their businesses. Preparing for a sales call with information about your station is a good idea, of course; but when you can provide potential clients with up-to-date information about their businesses, you really enhance your credibility and help improve your chances for success.

"Connect" with your customers!

Selling radio air time (or selling anything else) is intensely personal, and it is to your advantage to "connect" personally with your customers. In other words, you do not want customers to think of you as a sales robot.

A very effective way to connect is to find common ground with the client *outside* of your business relationship. With this in mind, it can be very useful to open your sales calls with discussions about children, sports, movies, restaurants, the weather … whatever works. (Avoid third-rail issues such as politics and religion.)

These conversations are great opportunities to create rapport with your customers and come fairly easily to individuals with natural sales skills, but this can be nerve-wracking when you're starting out. A good way to look for openers is to check out the client's office walls and desktop for photos, souvenirs, artwork, knick-knacks, etc., that provide clues as to his or her personal interests. For example, if the client has a Red Sox pennant or replica Patriots jersey on the wall, I know it is fairly safe to chat about the most recent developments with either team.

Of course, some clients don't want to "schmooze." They just want to get down to business, and they'll provide clues with their body language or the brevity of their responses to your friendly queries. They are basically telling you that they don't have time for small talk, and you must always respect their wishes and get right down to business

Personal connections do not work one-hundred percent of the t̲.
I know several sales professionals who are extremely skilled at connecting with clients on a personal basis, but the customers never buy! Astute representatives need to be able to quickly size up these types and save the personal interactions—if they are appropriate—for the golf course or service club meetings.

Here's the bottom line on connecting. I have had hundreds—maybe thousands—of clients during my career in radio sales. Some I really like personally and some I don't like at all. Whatever the case, they are all my customers, and my job is to provide them with an advertising plan that works and generate revenue for their businesses and mine.

Buying "you" vs. buying the product

I'll close out this chapter by with another adage that applies across the sales spectrum, whether you are selling appliances, automobiles, annuities, or air time: In many cases, the client is buying "you" and not the product. Most local business owners see legions of advertising salespeople every week. What can you do to differentiate yourself from the crowd? Is it the uniqueness of your station? The power of your personality? Your ability to solve a customer's problems?

I can't provide the answers to these questions. You will figure them out on your own with hard work, first-rate listening skills, and experience in getting to know your customers. Generally, you need to demonstrate a combination of all of the above and mix in a few intangibles as well.

*　　*　　*　　*

Again these are simply some basic business practices that I have developed, and they work for me. There is much more to say in these and related areas, and I have provided a number of resources in the appendix for those of you who wish to explore further.

For now, let's look at what goes on in the daily life of a radio sales professional.

CHAPTER 7

▼

A DAY OF "SELLING AIR"

So what, exactly, does an "air" salesperson do on a day-to-day basis to earn a living?

I've laid out the pieces of the puzzle for you in the previous chapters. Now let's put them all together. In this chapter, I'll provide you with a snapshot of what one day is like for someone in radio sales—a Monday, in this case. I hesitate to call it a "typical" day, because no two days selling air are ever alike, which to me is one of the attractive features of this career.

Before beginning, here's a word of advice. I am somewhat technophobic and prefer to go about my day with as little electronic gadgetry as possible. So I still plod along without a hand-held organizer (such as a Blackberry) or a laptop ... and I rarely use the text-message feature on my cell phone.

Because you are probably of a younger generation, all of these micro-devices are probably second nature to you, and I strongly advise you to take advantage of any or all of these technologies. Facility in the use of these items may provide you with an advantage in your interviews. These tools have rapidly become *de rigueur* among sales pros in all industries. In radio, they are especially valuable for the transmission of MP3 sound files across from your station to your customers.

With that in mind, here we go ...

6:45 a.m. to 8:00 a.m.—Taking Care of Myself First

I am a strong believer in physical well-being. Some kind of exercise is essential in my life, and my philosophy of "eat less (try to, anyway) and move more" helps address my lifelong weight management issues. So "moving more" is a good way to start any day.

Accordingly, on Monday morning this week, I worked out on my home exercise equipment. (Some days, when I am so motivated, I travel 15 minutes to the local YMCA and take advantage of the many more workout options that they offer.) In any event, my usual morning workout lasts from 30 to 45 minutes, followed by a shower, during which I begin to focus on the workday ahead.

On this day, I arrived in my office at about 8 o'clock.

8:00 a.m. to 8:30 a.m.—Organizing the Day

You may recall from Chapter 4 that I emphasized how important it is for you to organize your days and that you absolutely *must* have a plan in order to hold yourself accountable. With this in mind, I usually take about a half-hour each morning to organize my day.

On Mondays, the first thing I do is to check all my e-mails that arrived over the weekend. Very often, I will have checked these communications from home, mostly because I see my job as my own business, which means I need to maintain a 24/7 mindset.

When it comes to *responding* to e-mails, my office is usually the best venue because I have all of my data files right there. In addition, there may have been faxes that came in that require paperwork, signatures, or other responses. Many advertising agencies fax in orders and the account manager must sign and return them for confirmation.

My next task is to fill out weekly call sheets for the station's sales manager. In many offices, management requires that you produce call plans for the upcoming week: Whom you're going to call upon, and when; as well as an objective for each call (e.g., an annual contract or to gather specific information or check on ad results). Sales managers have different styles. Some will accept filled-out call sheets without much comment (especially if your sales numbers are good); while other managers will sit down with you and turn it into a coaching session. Either way, these are excellent methods for organizing your week.

On this particular Monday, I also compile a sales packet for a new automobile dealer whom I plan to call on. This requires writing a concise cover letter detailing my interest in working with them, summarizing my stations' merits, outlining what the station might be able to do in terms of advertising and promotion, and, finally, requesting an appointment. In addition to the letter, the packet included a coverage map, a station profile sheet, some statistical information about listener demographics, and the current rate card.

8:30 a.m. to 9:30 a.m.—Weekly Sales Meeting

8:30 is the time for the weekly sales meeting. This is the time when the sales team (the manager and all representatives) review and assess expectations for the day and week. If the manager has new sales aids, demographic data, Arbitron results, and rate cards, he will distribute them at this time.

These meetings can be highly creative and a lot of fun. This is because we often create new "products"—or packages—to promote to local businesses. Typically, these involve deals such as "buy three weeks of ads, get the fourth week free," or else we create a "third party promotion." This is when we offer bartered tickets or other prizes and incentives as part of a sponsor's promotion. For example, we might broadcast a winter-weather trivia question on behalf of a hardware store currently promoting snowblowers. The prize for the first person to call in with the correct answer might be two ski passes to a resort in Vermont.

The meeting might then move to an update on monthly budget progress for individuals and the sales team as a group. Each salesperson is informed of his or her progress in relation to sales goals and we review the station's overall situation in reference to the organization's total monthly goal.

These meetings can be highly motivational for the sales staff. This is a time for top performers to bask in the glory of their achievement, knowing that they must maintain their momentum in order to stay ahead of everyone else. A position at the bottom of the pack serves as incentive to move out of that position in the week ahead.

This is also a time when the sales manager might offer extra incentives, such as, "Everyone who makes goal by the end of this week gets a hundred-dollar bonus, and if the team makes goal by Friday, I'll treat everyone to lunch."

As I suggested above, the sales meeting can be an exhilarating experience if you are close to or beyond your goal—but a challenging (and potentially embarrassing) time if you are far from goal and holding the team back.

Usually, on Mondays we discuss the past weekend's station-related activities. These include live remote broadcasts, store openings, sponsored concerts, and so on. Typically, the different sales representatives will report on client feedback, listener comments, and how station and hired talent performed at weekend events.

Incidentally, for grand openings and other live remotes, we try to make sure to take pictures of the event. Usually, this means that a staff member (often a sales representative) brings along a digital camera and snaps away. Back at the station, we upload the frames onto a computer and send the best ones to the client along with a nice thank-you note. This is an especially effective goodwill gesture, especially when there was a good turnout

If the event didn't work out so well, this is a time for some constructive thinking to help ensure that the station—and the client—avoid pitfalls the next time around. More often than not, problems have to do with miscommunication between the salesperson, support staff, and the client, so you must always be very attentive regarding pre-remote setup and setting expectations for your clients.

Then we look ahead, checking on details for the current week's special promotions and live remotes. A key item on the agenda is to make certain that the program director and the promotions manager have all the "liners" and "mentions" ready and scheduled. These are the promotional announcements you often hear during breaks in the regular broadcast schedule (e.g., "During Winter Carnival Week, don't forget to stop by at a participating merchant to pick up your entry badge for all the events").

This is the time to confirm giveaway items, set contest parameters, and verify times, locations, staffing, client contacts, and so on. The more attention the team devotes to the process, the more likely it is that the event will be a rousing success.

If your sales manager is the cheerleader type, he or she will generally close the meeting with some motivational remarks or other words of inspiration designed to send everyone out the door determined to reach the weekly goal on that very day!

9:30 a.m. to 10:00 a.m.—"Prep" Time

After Monday sales meetings, I generally retreat to the privacy of my office to get ready to hit the road and start the *real* part of the sales professional's job. I use the time to enter new leads from the sales meeting, recheck my "to-do" list, and call clients to confirm my appointments for the day.

If you *do* pick up a new lead at the meeting, make it a point to follow up right away with a call to the prospect. I am a big believer in following up immediately and the sales managers love it when you do this. The secret is to let your manager know right away that you made the call and relay the results.

On this particular Monday, I stopped by the production booth to alert the production manager that one of my clients was due in at

10:15 to record a spot. (For this long-time client, it was not necessary for me to attend; for first-timers, I *always* sit in on the initial session to help establish the client's comfort level with the process.)

At about 9:50, I am out the door … to the local donut shop where I load up on coffee and pastries to deliver to the first client on today's call list; a home center and landscaping firm. This is a ritual with this particular client—one of the many favors I perform in order to help ensure that I stand out in this highly competitive arena. It is also nice that I have a small expense account. Thus, if I keep a record of these types of expenses, my company will cover them. During today's meeting I sit with the owner and discuss an upcoming ad campaign and schedule, and I commit to faxing him a "spec" spot and the order confirmation later that day

10:30 a.m. to 11:00 a.m.—First Visit with a New Prospect

At 10:15, I have an appointment with a new prospect—a women's clothing store that is about to open—to explore the benefits of radio advertising, with an eye toward developing an annual contract.

Obviously, a first meeting like this can take a myriad of shapes and forms. Sometimes, a visit like this can last 10 minutes because a client will simply tell you, "I need to be on the air tomorrow"; or else it can last up to an hour when you encounter a client who wants to relate his or her life story. The bottom line here is that you need to be flexible and know how to respond quickly to the client's needs. Generally, securing a longer-term contract is always better for you and your station, but this may not always be in the best interests of the client. Very often, starting with a short run of 30-second spots allows you to get your foot in the door while the client has the opportunity to measure results.

In this case, the client (part of a national chain) was interested in discussing their grand opening three weeks hence and wanted to identify the stations I represented and which of those would be most suitable for promoting the event. She expressed a wish for a live broadcast, and about a half hour of discussion gave me the name and numbers for her national marketing person, whom I promised to contact to discuss parameters for the event.

11:00 a.m. to 11:15 a.m.—A Little Self-Promotion

I immediately called the national marketing person on my cell phone and left her all my contact information. It never hurts to tally up brownie points with your manager, so while enroute to my next client, I checked in by with my boss to tell him how well the meeting went!

I also used this time to check my voice mail, but the only call was a request from a friend who wanted to set a tee time for the weekend ... I quickly returned the call to confirm that I was on board.

11:15 a.m. to 11:45 a.m.—A Cold-Call Check-In

My next stop was at a sports store to follow up on their current campaign promoting a big sporting goods sale. I know the owner well enough so that I can pretty much pop in anytime during the week.

On this day, I checked to see how the ads were working, if the client wanted any changes, and if they wanted to start thinking about their next campaign. I have found that it always helps to prompt certain clients to think ahead.

Unfortunately, even though the sale was going fairly well, my client informed me that he was going to try cable television for his next sale and was entertaining some thoughts of trying a direct-mail piece as well.

"I might not use radio for the next month or two," he said.

Of course, I reminded him that using even a little radio to add urgency to the sale would help, but I did not want to be too pushy. Despite the disappointment, my experience is that these clients inevitably return to the fold because ultimately radio advertising is an integral piece of successful marketing for local retail businesses. I have learned to practice patience in these situations, and my patience is generally rewarded.

Regular visits to your clients help sustain your relationships and prevent surprises. For example, you really don't want to walk in and find out that the client has decided to dump radio altogether in favor of a year-long newspaper campaign. Even worse, I would hate to walk in and find the business under new management when I had not been informed in advance. Believe me, these things happen.

11:45 a.m. to 12:30 p.m.—A Scheduled Check-In

Just before lunch hour, I stopped by at a furniture store to schedule an order for a new commercial run to begin on the following day. In this case, the client wanted to announce the addition of a new line they were carrying, and since they had a time-sensitive cooperative (or "co-op") reimbursement rearrangement with the manufacturer, the ads needed to run right away.

Because I have worked with this client for a long time, the meeting went very quickly. After writing down the client's instructions, I called the station right away—in the client's presence—and asked the traffic manager to immediately schedule the spots on the next day's log, and that I would have a sales order upon my return to the office. Making this call when I did demonstrated to the client that the station (usually) responds immediately to customer scheduling requests. It's just one more way to help promote solid relationships with your accounts.

When I got to my car, I left a voice mail with the production manager on the copy points for the ads, so that he could get a head start on writing the spots in time for the client to approve them before broadcast. In some cases, I actually fax in or e-mail some copy points right from the client's office so production can get a head start on the ad. (In rare situations, production staff is on vacation or otherwise unavailable, in which case the entire writing production responsibilities rest with the sales representative.)

12:30 p.m. to 1:30 p.m.—Client Lunch

After another quick check of my voice mail, it was off to my next stop ... a 12:30 lunch at a local Chinese restaurant with the owner/manager of the area's leading personnel firm. This was an important meeting for me because extension of the client's campaign would go a long way toward helping me reach my numbers for the week—and it would help the client generate traffic in an important time of year for his business.

After exchanging greetings, discussing our respective families, and recapping Sunday's New England Patriots football win, I shifted to a business theme. I suggested that the client produce a spot that would run for two weeks to focus on a special campaign around a new infusion of high-paying factory jobs they were listing. I also brought the client up to date on some forthcoming staff and programming changes at the station, (you never want a client to be "surprised").

I also planted the idea of having his company co-sponsor a road race and health fair at a local hospital that was coming up in a couple of months. This would be a natural tie-in for his business (the hospital is one of his clients), and I made a mental note to follow up on this idea in subsequent meetings.

When we adjourned at about 1:20, he agreed to the new spots for the factory job campaign. I was pumped up because I closed an important sale, which energized me for my next meeting ...

1:30 p.m. to 2:30 p.m.—First Meeting with a Real Estate Brokerage

At 1:30, I met with three principals from a regional real estate company that had never advertised on radio. Newspaper is usually the medium of choice in real estate—and more recently, the internet has become a preferred choice as well—, which is no surprise because photographs and virtual "tours" are essential draws for prospective buyers.

However, this company was looking for an edge over the competition and was exploring the concept of image advertising on radio (See Chapter 8). After querying for needs, goals, and expectations, I explained station demographics, programming themes, and the benefits of long-term image advertising.

Note that I mentioned "long-term." For selfish reasons, a long-term campaign generates more revenue for the station, more commissions for me and less need to go back to the client repeatedly to generate more business. But there is more to it than that. You can't be selfish. You want every sale to be a win-win proposition. Otherwise, the client will never come back.

When you think about it, effective image advertising is almost always a long-term proposition. After all, you want to implant an impression on the listener, and in radio, this usually requires repetition.

With that in mind, we talked about potential themes for a campaign, and discussed options, such as having the company president do the ads, or securing testimonials from satisfied homebuyers.

I left a sales kit, explained the rate card, and I secured a commitment to meet again at the same time next week.

2:30 p.m. to 3:00 p.m.—Collecting an Unpaid Bill

At 2:30, I stopped by a local wireless phone store to pick up a check for an advertising invoice that was almost 90 days out from the mailing date. This is not my favorite part of the job, but it's one that all sales reps must tackle every now and then. (Radio is unique, I think in this regard. In most business, there are collection types who deal with these issues—not the individuals who sold you the product.)

Let's face it, most companies don't like to part with their cash, and dragging payment out 45 to 60 days is not all that unusual in this business and many others. However, when 90 days approaches and the station has sent out numerous reminders (in addition, in some cases, to suspending ads), it's time to take action. When you get to 120 days, many broadcast companies will not pay commissions to their representatives.

I had called this particular client on the previous Thursday. They had promised that the check would be cut on Monday and that I could stop by and pick it up. Fortunately, they did have it. I thanked them, but frankly had no intention of pressing them for additional sales. I decided I would let them come to me in the near future. Their history of payment was not good, and the station was doing well at the time. I did not need the headaches.

3:00 p.m. to 4:00 p.m.—Back to the Station

I returned to the station at mid-afternoon to write the order for the personnel company's two-week campaign. I also wrote the copy for the first ad, for which I would provide the voiceover, handed it to the production manager, and scheduled an appointment the next morning to record the spot.

I also spent a few minutes with my sales manager talking about a potential strategy to secure an annual contract with this client, and reviewed the highlights of my meeting with the real estate group. This is generally productive because sales managers will have creative ideas on how to add value to your presentations, which in turn often prompts clients to buy.

Very often, the sales manager will advise you about new ideas that he or she may have picked up from a trade journal or seminar, and these can be very useful in adding a new spin to your proposal. This is another exciting part of the business of selling air—you have many opportunities to use your creativity.

I also used this time to check and respond to e-mails and phone calls.

4:00 p.m. to 5:15 pm.—Board Meeting

Once a month on a Monday afternoon, I attend a board meeting for a social service agency. I emphasized earlier that community service is a great way to make your "mark" in the community. Although I never discuss business at these meetings and related events, over time people get to know who I am and what I do, and business generally follows. In addition, I am helping enhance the quality of life for the families and individuals served by the agency. Again, it's win-win for everyone involved!

5:30 p.m. to 6:00 p.m.—Back at office ... and home!

I stopped in at the office one more time at about 5:30, checking e-mails and creating tomorrow's "to do" list.

On this day, I still had a leftover adrenaline rush from the personnel company meeting and was tempted to draft an annual contract ... but I decided that could wait until the next morning. Instead, I headed for the golf course for a quick nine holes before sunset on a beautiful early fall evening ... a great way to reward myself for a well-organized, productive, and very satisfying day.

They don't always proceed so well ... even the best representatives slog through some days with one rejection after another. Nevertheless, even on those days, I look for the silver lining. Perhaps I secured a commitment for a follow-up meeting, or I obtained a promising lead from someone whom I met on the street.

Always stay positive regardless of how the day pans out ... success will follow.

CHAPTER 8

▼

THE BUSINESS OF RADIO

To this point, this has pretty much been a "how to" book ... how you can land your first job in radio sales and increase your odds for success during your first few weeks on the job.

In this chapter, we'll drill down and look at the actual *business* of radio. We'll start by examining the wide variety of radio station formats. Later in the chapter, you'll learn about key business concepts of the broadcast industry that will provide you with baseline knowledge as you launch your career.

Radio station formats

As you know at this point, radio stations sell air—or more precisely, air *time*. But stations also sell *access* to consumers, and it is critical that advertisers obtain access to the *right* consumers: the specific demographic groups that are most likely to purchase the products and services being offered over the air.

With this in mind, a radio advertiser must take care to select the right format. The format is really the "brand identity" of the station and refers to the general type of programming it is best known for. The format determines the type of listener the station appeals to, or more broadly, the demographic sector of the population that the station delivers to advertisers.

Here, in alphabetical order, are brief descriptions of the most common general formats:

- *Adult Contemporary.* Often called "AC" in the industry, adult contemporary stations broadcast playlists of mainstream contemporary pop music which might focus on hip hop, hard rock, teen pop, or some mix. Subcategories in this format include:

  - "Christian AC," which limits musical offerings to contemporary spiritual and other family friendly tunes.

  - "Hot AC," also called "Adult Top 40," which focuses on current favorites as well as the more lively popular and rock music released during the past fifteen or twenty years

  - "Lite AC" (or "Soft AC"), which features more easy-going popular and rock music released during the past fifteen or twenty years designed to appeal to general listeners. This format recalls the "easy listening" style that is still popular in some areas.

  - "Urban AC," which can include any mix of such as rap, hip-hop, rhythm and blues, and soul; mix being dependent upon the age and ethnicity of the station's audience.

- *Classic Rock.* Classic rock stations play rock and folk-rock favorites released during the 1960s, 70s, and 80s. Most of these stations recreate to some degree the sound of album-oriented rock stations of that era and usually appeal to adults whose interest in this genre has carried over into their adult years.

- *Country.* Today's "country" music world includes a broad range of musical styles. Most country stations play popular music and former hits based on the traditional styles of the southern rural US and the American West. Country stations tend to thrive in those areas, but they have become mainstream in many other markets and often appeal to a very wide audience—from teens and college students to rural seniors.

- *Ethnic.* Programming at these stations is targeted toward a particular ethnic group, nation, or region. In the US, Hispanic stations are far and away the most prevalent stations of this type, but, depending upon geography and population density, you will also find many stations aimed specifically at the African-American market. In fact, data from a recent survey revealed that African-American radio is the most popular ethnic medium among Blacks in the United States.

- *News/Talk.* This format features round-the-clock news, and may also have regularly scheduled hosts who discussing current events and other topics, sometimes in the context of a particular political ideology. Talk programs frequently feature in-studio guests and allow listener call-ins. Within this general format, keep in mind that some stations may be virtually all news, while others are all talk. Another niche in this market is the all-sports station, which features sports news, sports talk, and live broadcasts of games.

- *Oldies.* These stations play popular, rock 'n roll, and rock hits from the 1950s, 60s and 70s. A few of these stations recreate the upbeat sound of popular AM stations of the period and tend to be popular with listeners who grew up during those decades. Oldies stations are different from classic rock stations, which are described below.

This list covers only the broadest category titles and does note even come close to including all the various niche markets and subcategories of radio formats that reach the US population. In fact, the Arbitron website lists the following *fifty-four* formats which that organization measures in its surveys:

- 80s Hits
- Active Rock
- Adult Contemporary (AC)
- Adult Hits
- Adult Standards/MOR
- Album Adult Alternative (AAA)
- Album Oriented Rock (AOR)
- All News
- All Sports
- Alternative
- Children's Radio
- Classical
- Classic Country
- Classic Hits
- Classic Rock
- Contemporary Christian
- Contemporary Inspirational
- Country
- Easy Listening
- Educational
- Ethnic
- Family Hits
- Gospel
- Hot AC
- Jazz
- Latino Urban
- Mexican Regional
- Modern AC
- New AC (NAC)/Smooth Jazz
- New Country
- News/Talk/Information
- Nostalgia
- Oldies
- Other
- Pop Contemporary Hit Radio
- Religious
- Rhythmic AC
- Rhythmic Contemporary Hit Radio
- Rhythmic Oldies
- Soft AC
- Southern Gospel
- Spanish Adult Hits
- Spanish Contemporary
- Spanish News/Talk
- Spanish Oldies
- Spanish Religious
- Spanish Tropical
- Spanish Variety
- Talk/Personality
- Tejano
- Urban AC
- Urban Contemporary
- Urban Oldies
- Variety

Obviously, selection of the right format is critical to the success of any radio advertising campaign. For example, if an advertiser's target audience is teens and college students, hot AC probably makes a lot more sense than easy listening.

Incidentally, in recent years I have had the advantage of working for an organization that operates a network stations with several different broadcast formats. This allows me and my colleagues a lot more flexibility than most competitors when meeting with prospective advertisers. We can't claim to reach *every* listener in the region, but it's a good bet that one of our formats will appeal to a good percentage of a particular advertiser's target audience.

Two kinds of ads—"impact" and "image"

When consulting with your clients on their radio advertising requirements, you'll quickly discover that just any old ad won't do. Individual "spots" (shorthand for commercials) must be carefully crafted and targeted to ensure that the messages help meet the advertiser's objectives.

With that in mind, take note that there are two basic types of radio ads: "impact" ads and "image" ads.

Impact advertising is the choice to make when an advertiser wants listeners to take action *now*. Usually, this means that there's a sale, a special event, a concert, a grand opening, a theatrical performance, or something similar that requires a consumer to take fast action in order to secure the benefits of whatever is being promoted. Impact ads for sales are most often used by automobile dealerships, furniture stores, fast-food restaurants, supermarkets, beverage stores, and so on. Also, impact ads are usually big on *features* and *benefits*. For example, "The new Magic Vision 48-inch, high-definition TV with magna-sound [features] will let you watch this weekend's big game just like you're in the stadium [benefit]."

From a strategic perspective, the usual approach with impact advertising is for the advertiser to purchase as many ads as the budget allows as far in advance of the event as possible. Usually, one week of high concentration 30- or 60-second commercials generates sufficient traffic for a sale event at a retail store. For events like concerts and festivals— especially those that have a good chance of selling out—two to three weeks of the same might make more sense, budget permitting.

Image advertising, on the other hand does not ask the listener to take an immediate, specific action, nor do they hammer home features and benefits. Instead, image ads promote the general "look and feel" of a product or service, rather than a direct call to action. Image advertising is commonly used for differentiating competitive marketers from one another. Image ads usually focus on the listener's lifestyle and work not through persuasion ("Buy *now!* Sale ends Sunday!"), but through suggestion or association ("Stunning hilltop luxury dining with spectacular views of the area's lakes and mountains ... ").

Most image advertising attempts to establish a brand identity that the consumer can associate with. One of the most effective (and at the same time, most despised) visual image campaigns of all time is the Marlboro Man, which did a very effective job of promoting the image of rugged, western-style masculine individualism.

On radio, image advertising has been effectively implemented over the years by Burger King ("Have it your way."), Maxwell House Coffee ("Good to the last drop!"), Pepsi-Cola ("For those who think young."), Chevrolet ("Like a rock!"), and BMW ("The ultimate driving machine"), and Motel 6 ("We'll leave the light on for ya", one of the most successful image campaigns of all time).

While short-term impact ads are usually most effective, image advertising is generally more effective over the long term. But at the same time, the challenges facing the image advertiser are more complex.

When developing an image campaign with a client, my first step is ask three questions that address the three "musts" of image advertising:

1. *What is your unique selling proposition, or "USP"?* This is the *one* factor more than anything else that differentiates the client from the competition. It could relate to price, service, location, convenience, or atmosphere (as for a restaurant or hotel). This factor needs to be noted in every image ad, either directly ("closer to metropolitan Boston than any other major ski resort"); or indirectly ("... set on 75 lush, rolling acres, with state-of-the art wine-making and distillation facilities, an exceptional wine and gift shop, an on-premises brewery, and a gourmet restaurant").

2. *How can you "cut through the noise"?* Here the radio advertiser has a broad range of choices: customer testimonials, two-voice dialogue,

humor, drama, or an effectively-produced jingle or "tag" that appears in every ad. A winning image ad must demand the attention of the listener despite the distraction of other "noise" emanating from the station's broadcasts.

3. *What frequency best matches your budget?* Whether the budget allows a run of 20 to 30 ads per week or just once a day five days per week on morning news—or something in between—consistent exposure of an image message is necessary to penetrate the consciousness of the listener. Here's my rule of thumb: When clients gets sick of hearing their own image ads, the average listener is just beginning to absorb the message.

Duration—15, 30, or 60 seconds

A few paragraphs back I suggested that 30- or 60-second commercials make the most sense for retail impact ads. So let's examine the options that are available. Stations usually offer commercials that run for 15, 30 or 60 seconds. (Some stations also offer 5- or 10-second "mentions" and even 1-second "blinks.")

Obviously, 60-second ads cost more, so they generate more revenue-per-ad for the station (and the sales representative) ... but the one-minute ad might not always be the best option for the client.

It's true that 60-second ads are currently popular—especially among big national advertisers—and they actually cost only about 20% more than 30-second ads. The rationale behind a 60-second ad is that it gives the advertiser plenty of time to deliver the promotional message and comfortably mention the advertiser's name at least three times, which is the rule of thumb.

But consider this: Why not buy double your exposure for only 20% more cost? McDonald's, for instance, has researched the fact that that the human brain actually "listens" to an ad for about 22 seconds, so you will sometimes hear two 30-second ads back-to-back in two consecutive commercial breaks. This is called "piggybacking."

McDonald's generally uses different voices and possibly different theme music, but whatever the tactics, the ads "trick" listeners into thinking that they have heard two different ads. Thus, the advertiser delivers multiple impressions instead of prompting the subconscious mind to tune out after the first ad.

Of course, McDonald's has a huge budget, which allows for creative ads and aggressive scheduling; and the results have been obvious over the years as they have maintained a worldwide leadership position in the fast food market sector. Incidentally, with the exception of frequent short-term promotional tie-ins with family-oriented movies (usually a free theme toy with the purchase of a Happy Meal®), McDonald's tends to thrive on image advertising. Their image ads run frequently in a variety of media, and each of us can probably recall at least one McDonald's jingle or promotion that has been imprinted in our brains for eternity.

Occasionally, 60-second ads work well for an impact campaign. For example, if an advertiser is promoting a concert or music festival, it might be a good idea to highlight the "draw" performers and play cuts of their music. For a play or movie, a few lines of intriguing or humorous dialogue usually generate interest. These approaches can be very effective in creating excitement, setting expectations, and prompting action.

For sales and other retail advertising, however, 30-second ads—or even 15-second spots—tend to work best *if* the client schedules them for frequent runs. If an advertiser runs full-page or insert newspaper campaigns that heavily promote price specials, then a good 30-second ad can refer listeners to the ads, highlight one or two special deals, and mention the business name at least twice (the rule of thumb on 30's). Promoting a laundry list of price points on radio doesn't work. There's too much detail for the listener to absorb. It's a turnoff.

Thus, in a special-pricing situation a good ad might say something like: "Diamond's Bookstore, this weekend only on selected best sellers: Buy one, get the second at half price. See Friday's ad in the *Clar-*

ion-Ledger for available titles … Authors include James Patterson, Danielle Steele, John Grisham, and many others …" and so on. For anyone in the market for a good novel or a gift for a friend, this ad would probably be very effective. Even the phrase "half price" is almost certain to draw attention.

Sixty second ads can also be impact oriented. A well-done ad for a concert or a show, mixing in different exciting musical selections or bits from a play, often encourages listeners to show up. Painting a picture of an exciting evening out might get people to respond immediately, and thus 60 seconds can be used effectively for impact. The automotive industry is fond of using 60-second ads to not only promote a sale but also provide examples of different vehicles that might appeal to listeners. In other words, 60-second ads can be used for impact *and* image.

If the client has a lot to say, choose between one 60-second version or two 30-second versions, splitting the information between the two and rotating the two different versions. If using this strategy, you'll want to promote continuity and brand recognition, so make certain that the voice, musical theme and general look-and-feel are similar. (You can, of course, rotate two or more 60-second ads in the same cycle as well.)

Regarding 15-second spots, quick-hitting ads make sense for the advertiser who wants to create frequency and name recognition at lower per-spot cost. A skilled sales rep can work with an account to identify the critical information that must be the focus of a brief commercial. It's difficult to create 15-second commercials that have impact, but the scheduling of several 15-second "tags" in support of a campaign that features 60's and/or 30's can be a very effective way to supporting a campaign's main message.

Scheduling the spots

Efficient scheduling of a client's ads is critical to the success of any campaign. Every advertiser's objective is to reach the maximum number of listeners at a fair cost. With this in mind, it's important to be aware of the radio listening tendencies of consumers.

Let's start with "drive times." Drive time is considered the optimum time for radio broadcasting. Morning drive time refers to the hours when listeners wake up, prep their coffee and breakfast, primp and preen, and head to work or school. Afternoon drive time includes the time when commuters head home from work before evening mealtime.

Although stations vary in the precise definitions of their drive times, morning drive usually runs from 6 a.m. to 10 a.m., and evening drive time from 3 p.m. to 7 p.m. These are the periods where the number of listeners is highest and commercial radio can charge the most for advertising. (Some stations start their morning drive blocks as early as 5 a.m., and their afternoon slots as early as 2 p.m.—a shrewd method for generating more advertising dollars).

Obviously, in major metropolitan markets where commuters jam the highways and public transportation, radio advertisers have a captive audience, and investment in drive-time advertising makes a lot of sense. But what about small towns? In small towns and rural areas, as is the case in my territory, there are no packed freeways—no traffic jams at all, in fact. So does targeting the drive-time audience make sense?

I like to think so, because countless individuals and families are still listening to the radio while they are having their coffee, reading their morning papers, checking their e-mails, and driving to work or school. The same thing is true at the end of the day. The radio is usually on when folks are returning home from their busy days.

So, for the advertiser with a reasonable budget I generally recommend drive-time placement at the core of a campaign—that is the best way to reach a maximum number of listeners. In some cases, I may suggest drive-time advertising as part of a Total Audience Plan, or "TAP." This arrangement provides the advertiser with one-third of their commercials in drive time; a third mid-day; and a third at night.

There is another designation called "run of station," or ROS. Under this arrangement, a client's spots are scheduled at the station's discretion any time of the day, any day of the week. This usually makes sense when an advertiser wants to promote a sale or event at the last minute or simply has a low budget and is willing to take what is available.

For some advertisers, daily sponsorship of a regular show, such as Paul Harvey, the stock report, or sports updates, might make sense, since these broadcasts usually have a regular listenership. The same concept works if your station broadcasts the entire schedule of a big league sports team. For example, my network broadcasts all 162 regular season Boston Red Sox games every year (plus a few playoff games, if we are lucky). Because interest in the Red Sox is very high, the purchase local ads for these broadcasts is very popular in my area.

However clients choose to schedule their spots, always keep in mind the importance of repetition. Most listeners cannot automatically recall a radio commercial's message until they have heard it four, five, or six times. If they miss an address, a key date, a price, or an address the first time, they tend to want to hear the ad again so that they can capture the key information. Thus, for impact advertising, high frequency over a short period of time is usually the best strategy. Lower frequency over a longer period of time should be reserved for image ads.

Ratings, ratings, ratings

A lot of advertisers want proof that their commercials actually reach people who listen to the radio, and for that the industry provides you with Arbitron ratings.

Arbitron is a radio audience research company that collects and publishes data in a similar manner that Neilson Media research does for television. Data is useful for estimating audience size, determining listener demographics, identifying listener trends throughout the day and week, and comparing listenership among stations in a market area.

Traditionally, Arbitron has collected data by selecting a random sample of the population in a region and asking houshold members to maintain diaries describing each station and program listened to. Individuals in each household aged 12 and older is provided a diary and is expected to track radio listening for an assigned week.

At the end of the week, the participants mail the completed diaries to Arbitron, and Arbitron selects different random samples for subsequent weeks. Arbitron's surveys in major market areas are divided into four key ratings periods that correspond to the seasons. Thus, the Arbitron ratings books are referred to as the Spring Book, Summer Book, and so on.

Arbitron evaluates listener habits from 6:00 until midnight from Monday through Friday, 48 weeks per year. After collection, the survey results are marketed to radio networks, individual stations, and advertising agencies.

Major ratings categories include:

- *CUME*—the cumulative number of unique listeners over a period

- *Average quarter hour* (AQH)—the average number of people listening every 15 minutes

- *Time spent listening (TSL)*—the amount of time a participant spent listening to each radio station at one time before changing the station or turning the radio off

- *Demographic breakdown*—listener breakdown by age and gender

With the advent of sophisticated electronic devices and the desire to provide more accurate data, Arbitron recently introduced the Portable People Meter (PPM). The PPM is a wearable portable device, similar to a cell phone, or a pager, that electronically records the listening behavior and history of a single participant throughout the day for several months. The PPM is currently being rolled out in the top ten US media markets. I suspect it will be quite awhile before the new device hits small rural markets, such as the one I sell in in western Massachusetts.

Speaking of my area, my primary sales territory, Franklin County, is considered a non-metro "submarket" by Arbitron. Arbitron actually publishes a Franklin County "book" twice a year, and I use it to provide relevant information to my clients and prospects. There is a similar book for adjacent Hampshire Country, then a larger—four-times-a-year presentation for the larger Springfield market area, both of which impact stations in my network.

Truthfully, these ratings carry little weight with local, small-business advertisers. After all, the sample size for Franklin County—with 65,000 residents—is around a hundred people. National advertisers have more experience with Arbitron, and I have found the "Arbies" to be more useful with companies such as McDonald's, Wendy's, and Subway, that are willing to purchase ads from stations with much smaller audiences than they find in the major metro areas.

The bottom line is that, rating book or no rating book, if you create solid relationships with your customers, help them create campaigns that match their specific needs, and the station delivers results, the numbers mean very little anyway.

For those of you who are interested, the appendix features a sample page from an Arbitron ratings report.

*   *   *   *

This chapter has provided you with basic background information on the business of radio that will, at a minimum, provide you with a good foundation before your job interviews. If you can demonstrate knowledge about impact versus image ads, drive times, run-of-station, and cumes, you will definitely make an impression on station management. You will, of course, learn more about these concepts in your on-the-job training.

CHAPTER 9

▼

TOP 10 WAYS TO JUMP-START YOUR CAREER IN RADIO SALES

I hope that this book has provided you with an adequate introduction to what a career in radio sales is all about. I think you've seen that it is a challenging profession that offers a great deal of intellectual and financial rewards to those who are successful.

If you are thinking about a career in radio sales—or just starting out—I hope that my thoughts have provided sufficient encouragement to take the next step. If you have just been hired and are reading this book as part of your orientation, you now have an idea of what lies ahead.

At the end of every training program that I have attended, the facilitator has always made it a point to briefly present some motivational remarks to participants. My motivational remarks to you are presented in the form of ten techniques that I believe helped me achieve and maintain a high level of success during my radio sales career.

Read and apply them, and you'll have a jump-start on your own successful career as a radio sales representative.

1. Step out of your comfort zone.

This is the most important tip that I share with every individual whom I mentor or anyone else who asks how they can enhance or accelerate their career advancement. If you want to be successful working in an organization for and with other people, one of the best ways to control your own destiny is to start learning and doing things that you are not necessarily comfortable with. Very often this means taking charge and completing tasks that others in the organization may not want to do.

I can't stress this enough. Whether it's creating PowerPoint graphics presentations that your manager cannot (or will not) do, delivering invoices to clients, calling on difficult clients, or helping out at weekend events, there are countless ways to enhance your visibility and score points with your employer.

This does not guarantee advancement or job security, but when the manager starts to believe that the business can't function without you, you certainly have a significant advantage.

2. Ask for help.

Always take the time to communicate with your manager and ask for help or mentoring. I noted earlier that new sales reps are sometimes "thrown to the wolves" on the day they start their new job. This means that they are interacting with potential clients without a good base of knowledge and experience. When you think about it, it is highly counterproductive for management to manage newcomers in this manner.

Regardless of the situation, it's your responsibility to develop a good relationship with your general manager or sales manager and obtain from them the support you need. When I was learning, I was constantly in my manager's office asking questions, submitting creative ideas, and looking for direction. She was not always pleased with my persistence, but eventually she acknowledged the results of her investment in coaching.

3. Know the product *and* the business inside out.

This is true in any sales position. The more intelligent and you feel and sound, the more confident you'll be, and the more credibility you will have in the eyes of your clients.

This means that you must know:

- Your station's advertising rates for all the key packages and critical time periods

- Current Arbitron ratings for your station and the competition for critical time periods

- Demographics of your station's listener base

- Billing procedures, including discounts for early payments

- You station's daily broadcast schedule

A knowledgeable sales representative is a credible sales representative. There's nothing like a positive, confident attitude in the sales business. Clients will feed off your confident, self-assured nature and will *want* to work with you to develop solutions for their business challenges.

4. Know your client's business.

In-depth knowledge of your *clients'* business operations also helps enhance your credibility as a sales representative. Whether it's automobiles, furniture, entertainment, fast food, insurance, sporting goods, organic farming—whatever—if you expect the customer to purchase air time, you had better know *why* the customer needs it.

There are endless resources available to you—especially those on the Internet—that can help you get information about almost any business you want to learn about. Simply use any search engine. For example, I just ran a search for "appliances," and I could have spent the next hour learning about refrigerators, freezers, air conditioners, venting systems, stoves and ovens, microwaves, and a whole lot more.

When you plan your first call to an appliance store, do exactly the same thing and take the time to research products, features, benefits, pricing, and so on. Of course, if a prospective client sponsors its own website, research it front to back before your first call.

When you can talk intelligently with your clients about their businesses, you're well on your way toward developing a mutually rewarding relationship with long-term advertisers.

5. Listen, listen, and then listen more

I mentioned earlier that listening skills are critical in radio sales. Clients want to be heard. They will say they don't have the time to talk with you, but if you can secure a commitment for an appointment—or a lunch meeting—with no interruptions, you will be surprised at the extent to which they will discuss their business history, successes, failures, goals, challenges, dreams, and so on.

If you like to talk (like I do), it's not always easy to just sit back and listen to what someone else has to say, but it's absolutely essential if you want to maintain solid business relationships with your clients.

6. Manage time wisely

Effective time management leads to more contacts in the field, which leads to more sales. As I noted earlier, its very useful to have at least one to-do list to help stay on top of all of your responsibilities. Choose one of two times a day to answer phone calls and deal with e-mails—don't allow random phone calls and e-mail to interrupt other activities. Remember, too, that you will also have appointments, meetings, and a ton of paperwork to deal with. And group your sales calls geographically so that you are not zig-zagging all over your territory wasting time in your car.

It is very easy to become distracted, confused, and sometimes over-whelmed by all the tasks that a radio sales profession must accomplish in one day. That's why you need to be very conscious of—even selfish about—how you spend your time. It's your responsibility to plan every day and have it evolve the way *you* want it to.

Think of it this way: You are actually managing your *own* business within the broader business of the station that employs you. If you want your business to be successful, you must manage your time effi-ciently!

7. Forget about time off and vacation (for awhile)

I just mentioned that, as a radio sales professional, you are in effect managing your own business. As is the case with any startup enterprise, the hours are usually long and arduous in the early going. If you have a track record of eying the clock and leaving as quickly as you can at the end of a work shift, radio sales is probably not the best career choice—unless you are willing to change your habits.

If you want to be successful in radio sales, think of it as both a career and a lifestyle—not just a "job." In the beginning, long hours are typi-cally necessary. They are an investment in your future success. The investment pays off later in terms of a handsome income, as well as flexible hours and time off for vacations.

8. Take extra good care of your clients

It's so much easier keeping a good client happy then to spend time try-ing to locate and "convert" new clients. Your clients are your custom-ers, and (as with any business), good customer service is essential for success.

With this in mind, treat your best clients to lunch from time to time. Send them thank you notes and e-mails. Volunteer to help them out when it is appropriate to do so (e.g., helping them secure props for a window display). Send them copies of favorable newsclips about their businesses. Congratulate them when you see their children's names mentioned in the paper for academic or athletic achievements. Basically, do whatever it takes to have them feel appreciated and special.

Very often I deliver coffee and donuts to client offices around town, or pizzas or a sandwich tray at lunchtime. You may occasionally knock heads with your manager when you present an expense check for these treats, but the payoff comes in revenues for your station. I believe that providing extra attention to clients sets you apart from the competition. My observations suggest that too many reps take their clients for granted. Don't let this happen to you.

9. Hold yourself accountable

As a mature adult, you alone are responsible for your successes and failures. Past failures and tough current circumstances simply represent steppingstones for greater achievement.

Don't forget that the one reason why you were hired is to generate business for your station and its customers—now, *that's* opportunity

You have probably observed in life—or even experienced—how easy it is for people to blame others for their own shortcomings. In my career, I've heard such excuses as, "My manager never gives me any good leads" or "I never got any training."

Learn to recognize when you—and others—are simply making excuses. As a professional, you must be acutely aware of your own strengths and weaknesses. Determine what steps you need to take to improve your sales, your career, and your situation. Take action and implement steps with an eye on crafting the future as you see it. Visualization is a powerful tool. Create your vision, then take steps to make it come true.

Also, maintaining your integrity and character is critical in sales. If you don't have the answer, tell the customer and then follow up with the appropriate information. Sell honestly and ethically.

It's often tempting to bend the rules. I've seen it happen. It rarely pays off. So forget about it. Don't risk losing a customer. Always act responsibly.

10. Be creative, have fun

You are hired as a broadcast sales representative because station management believes that you can handle the job and generate business for the company. No one else has your personality and God-given gifts and talents, so make the most of them.

Always make it a point to have fun and enjoy what you do with this job. Don't be afraid to implement interesting ideas, strategies, promotions, and campaigns that you and your customers—and *their* customers will enjoy.

Some sales experts have told me that imagination is more important than intellect. I think there is a lot of truth in this. When you combine your knowledge of radio with what you learn about your clients' business and add a little imagination, there are few limits to what you can achieve in radio advertising. When it comes to your imagination in this business, the sky is the limit!

*　　　*　　　*　　　*

My final advice to you is this: Apply what you have learned here. Seek the advice of others in the business. Consult the resources listed in the appendix (and perform your own search). Check out the opportunities in your area … and have a *great* career.

▼

Lessons learned: When a client says "No!"

(It does not necessarily mean "No")

As I noted earlier in this book, radio sales representatives (like all sales professionals) must deal with rejection on a daily basis. It comes with the turf. Sometimes prospects are tactful and diplomatic when they decline to do business with you. Other times they are ... shall I say more "direct."

But still ... things change, as demonstrated by the three anecdotes that follow:

(1) "I never want to buy another ad again!

One Monday morning about five years into my career, I walked into a downtown retail store. I did not have an appointment, but I thought I had fairly good relationships with the store owner and his manager.

I always anticipated some sarcastic banter with this person. That's just the way he is. I can assert myself when I need to, but I usually let this guy play his "game," and I went along with it.

Let's call him "Bruno." On this particular day, Bruno was obviously off to a bad start and it had nothing to do with me or the radio station. When I entered the store, he looked up and said, "What the hell are *you* doing here?" I knew right away that he was in an extraordinarily foul mood. I mumbled some barely audible response, hoping I could find a graceful way to exit the store.

No chance.

"We don't want any advertising and we will *never* buy radio ads again!"

Hmmmm …

At this point I tried to say something positive and non-threatening and make light of the situation but he wasn't having any of it.

"I don't care, never come in here again for advertising!" he almost shouted.

It was clear there was no room for civil discourse at the moment, so I left the store stunned, confused, angry, and hurt.

How I could I not take this affront personally, especially since I had spent a fair amount of time nurturing the relationship. I retreated to my office and tried to elicit some sympathy from my manager and colleagues at the station. Apparently, they all had their own problems on that day, so the situation festered for the rest of the day and into the evening.

First thing Tuesday morning, I answered a phone call. It was the same store owner who was inexcusably rude to not 24 hours before.

"Can you come right over and see me?" he asked. "I have an ad and I want to get it on the air right away!"

He spoke mater-of-factly with no emotion and no mention of our interaction the day before.

I left immediately for his store. Again, there was no acknowledgment that anything unusual had occurred previously. With no prodding from he, he placed an unusually high-volume order. His first ad was on the air the following day, and he continued as a strong advertiser for many years thereafter.

We never discussed the incident. I guess that in his mind it never happened.

In any event, this experience taught me a very valuable lesson: Do not take anything like this personally. This event helped me to understand that my clients have problems and daily ups and downs just like anyone else.

It also reinforced another one of my rules for radio sales: Until someone says "I absolutely don't want to buy ads on your station," I *still* assume that he or she is a potential clients. I'll allow prospects to say no many times before I give up on them. It's surprising how many times someone will make the "buy" decision long past the time when you perhaps should have given up and moved on.

This does not mean spending tons of time on clients who have no reason (or no money) to buy radio. It just means that very often a sales obstacle simply represents another sales opportunity.

(2) "We don't buy radio! Period!"

"We don't buy radio! Period! My father-in-law has run the business for twenty-five years. We never bought radio ads and we do fine without them. There's no reason to start now."

Thus spoke the manager of a local landscape business and retail nursery. Having shopped at the store and considered its business potential, I believed that the enterprise was severely undermarketed. The business was well known on the commercial side among landscape architects and contractors, but their facility was somewhat out of the way and consumers did not generally know much about it.

To his credit, the manager allowed me to complete a customer needs assessment (or "CNA"—see Chapter 4). When reviewing the assessment, I zeroed in on the fact that, unlike competitors in the area, this company grew virtually all of its own stock; so they had a unique selling proposition that could serve as a great "hook" for an ad campaign.

It also helped that I hired this firm to do some of my own landscaping, and the crew did an exceptional job. I made it a point to express my satisfaction to the manager.

Shortly afterwards, we agreed to test a campaign in which I did a first-person testimonial as a satisfied customer. We included a catch-phrase, "We grow almost all of what we sell."

The results rolled in right away. During the first few weeks that the ad ran, I received more feedback on this campaign than on any other for which I had done the voiceover. More importantly, the client enjoyed walk-ins from countless new customers who heard the ads on the radio, and retail sales increased significantly.

This client, like the one in the previous anecdote, became a loyal long-term advertiser. This was a situation in which I was able to help a new client with the right product deliver the right message at the right time—with the right results!

This doesn't happen all the time, but it's just one more example of why it often makes sense to look beyond a prospect's first "No." If you can spot a need and come up with a common-sense solution, then chances are you will win the business!

(3) Know when to fold 'em

It probably won't be too far into your sales career when run into the classic "rate grinder." This is a prospective customer who seems to know what rate every station should charge. This is the customer's way of intimidating you enough so that you'll cave in on your rates which, depending upon station policy, may or may not be negotiable. Here's a story that illustrates what just might work for you in that type of situation:

This happened during my rookie year in broadcast sales. My manager—as sales managers often do to "test" the new kid on the block—handed me a list of prospects that had rebuffed all previous efforts to advertise with the station.

One of these accounts was a local automobile dealer. It's important to understand that automotive businesses are among the most lucrative accounts for both radio and television stations. Any representative who can add one or two auto dealers to his or her business portfolio early on is definitely off to a great start.

Anyway, let's call the auto dealer in question X Auto Sales. I called up Mr. X to schedule an appointment, and he graciously invited me to his office on the following day. We spent about 20 minutes discussing his business. This was basically a time for me to ask the ask probing questions to determine where radio might fit into his advertising mix. whether or not the radio products I had to sell would fit his needs. After that session of questions and answers, we decided that a campaign on my station was a prefect match for X Auto's needs.

The next step was to determine spot frequency and map out a schedule—and to tally up the total cost. When Mr. X. noted the bottom line price he scornfully shouted that the rates were ridiculously high and that he would never pay them. He said they were the highest rates he had ever seen with any station in the area.

In truth, the rates that were attached to this schedule were the lowest rates available based on the number of spots and length of contract, and in my mind they were fair and reasonable. I explained this to the client, and the client essentially told me that I was a crook to ask for these rates.

At this point in time I "folded" my hand, thanked him for his time, and headed for the door. He quickly jumped up from his seat and blocked my exit.

"Where are you going?" he asked.

"On to my next call," I said.

"Well, hold on," he said, beckoning me back into the office. "Apparently you think I'm trying to rake you over the coals by charging you too much. Is that right?"

"Yes," I responded. "That is certainly the impression."

"Well, I was just testing you," he said. "And you passed!"

He then signed the contract, X Auto enjoyed the benefits of a great advertising campaign, and I earned a healthy commission.

In this situation, the adage "Know when to fold' em" proved to be a winning tactic. It won't win the business every time, but it is worth keeping in the back of your mind to implement it when it is appropriate to do so.

APPENDIX B

▼

CUSTOMER NEEDS
ASSESSMENT

Company: _____ **Contact:** _____ **Date:** _____
Address: _____ **Phone:** _____ **Fax** _____
E-mail _____

How did you get into the _____ business?	Customer Demographics:
	Current: Male _____% Female _____%
How long in business?	Desired: Male _____% Female _____%
	Current: ☐ 18-24 ☐ 25-34 ☐ 35-44 ☐ 45-54 ☐ 55-64 ☐ 65+
	Desired: ☐ 18-24 ☐ 25-34 ☐ 35-44 ☐ 45-54 ☐ 55-64 ☐ 65+
No. and location of branches:	
	Customer Income:
	Current: ☐ <$20K ☐ $20-40K ☐ $40-60K ☐ $60-75K ☐ $75K+
Business advantages:	Desired: ☐ <$20K ☐ $20-40K ☐ $40-60K ☐ $60-75K ☐ $75K+
• Why do customers come to you?	
	Marketing Area:
• What do you offer that competitors can't or won't?	Current: ☐ Regional ☐ Local ☐ Neighborhood
• What makes your business unique? (Positioning)	Desired: ☐ Regional ☐ Local ☐ Neighborhood
Major competitors?	Hours:
• Who are your competitors?	Peak hours:
• Why do customers go there?	Best days:
• What is their largest competitive advantage?	Dates and names of all major sales events:
• What is your biggest competitive disadvantage?	_____
	_____
Co-op Vendor:	_____
• The major sources of advertising support I've uncovered are…	_____
	_____
• What are other possible sources of cooperative advertising funds?	_____
	Two strongest sales events and why they are the most successful:
Are you taking advantage of discretionary vendor support?	

Customer Needs Assessment (continued)

Financing:	Annual Budget:
• Bank cards accepted? (Which ones?)	
• Revolving plan?	
• 90 Same as cash?	What commercials do you find most appealing?
Image: Current: ☐ Low price ☐ Large inventory ☐ Service ☐ Other Desired ☐ Low price ☐ Large inventory ☐ Service ☐ Other	What type or style of commercial would best depict your business?
What is the biggest misconception of your business?	☐ Comedy ☐ Highly creative ☐ Slice-of-life ☐ Straight read

Rank by order of importance to your business (Circle):

	Unimportant								Very Important	
Billboard	1	2	3	4	5	6	7	8	9	10
TV	1	2	3	4	5	6	7	8	9	10
Radio	1	2	3	4	5	6	7	8	9	10
Newspaper	1	2	3	4	5	6	7	8	9	10
Direct mail	1	2	3	4	5	6	7	8	9	10
Magazines/trade pub'ns	1	2	3	4	5	6	7	8	9	10
Telemarketing	1	2	3	4	5	6	7	8	9	10

Do you have an agency?

What's the single greatest problem you face today?

Single most important advertising medium?

• What do you like best?

• What do you like least?

• If you could, how would you change or improve the medium?

Others involved in planning and implementing advertising program:

How annual advertising budget is spent (%):

___Billboard
___TV
___Radio
___Newspaper
___Direct mail
___Magazines/trade pub'ns
___Telemarketing

Could we both benefit from my asking these questions of others?

Advertising frequency (How often)?

_____Billboard
_____TV
_____Radio
_____Newspaper
_____Direct mail
_____Magazines/trade pub'ns
_____Telemarketing

• *Thank you for the opportunity to meet with you today to learn more about you and your business.*

• *Over the next few days I'll be comparing the information you've shared with a variety of sales marketing data from our research department.*

• *As we conduct this research, should I be looking for information on any other areas of specific interest to you?*

• *Let's get together on (_____) to review what I find and share some ideas on how you might maximize your marketing and **advertising effectiveness**.*

APPENDIX C

▼

SAMPLE ARBITRON SURVEY SHEET

When you hear a radio, write down:

TIME

Write the time you start listening and the time you stop. If you start at one time of day and stop in another, draw a line from the time you start to the time you stop.

STATION

Write the call letters, dial setting or station name. If you don't know, write down the program name. If you listen over the Internet or to a satellite radio service, please include the station name or channel number.

Mark AM or FM. AM and FM stations can have the same call letters. Make sure you mark ☒ the right box.

THURSDAY

Time		Station	Place					
Start	Stop		AM	FM	At Home	In a Car	At Work	Other Place
6:45	7:15	KGTU		X	X			
7:15	7:40	100.0		X		X		
9:30		KEM	X					X
	12:00							
2:15	2:35	Alpha Satellite - Ch 256		X				
4:20	4:25	Internet - WGXP		X				
7:00	8:50	Jo Country Show	X					X
11:30	12:15	Robin 985		X	X			

If you didn't hear a radio today, please mark ☒ here. ☐

PLACE

Mark where you listen:
▪ at home
▪ in a car
▪ at work
▪ other place

Write down all the radio you hear. Carry your diary with you starting Thursday, Date 1a.

No listening? If you haven't heard a radio all day, mark ☒ the box at the bottom of the page.

©2006 Arbitron, Inc., reprinted with permission

The grid shown here illustrates how a participant in an Arbitron ratings survey is instructed to fill out his or her survey card. Results from a selected sample size are compiled to produce audience ratings. High ratings can help support a radio salesperson's presentation because they demonstrate that the station reaches a substantial number of listeners in certain demographic groups for certain time periods. Stations with consistently high ratings can generally charge more for air time.

As of 2007, Arbitron is in the process of replacing its manual diary system with the PPM™ system, which features hand-held electronic devices.

APPENDIX D

▼

ARBITRON SURVEY
RESULTS

AQH Share for Persons 12+, Mon-Sun 6AM-Mid—Springfield MA

Station	Format	FA04	WI05	SP05	SU05
WAQY-FM	Classic Rock	8.1	7.0	9.9	7.6
WHYN-AM	News Talk Information	7.8	6.2	7.7	8.9
WMAS-FM	Adult Contemporary	7.1	7.6	7.6	8.9
WPKX-FM	Country	6.7	7.6	7.3	6.3
WHYN-FM	Hot Adult Contemporary	6.6	7.2	6.2	7.6
WLZX-FM	Active Rock	3.5	3.8	4.3	3.7
WZMX-FM	Rhythmic Contemporary Hit Radio	6.6	5.8	4.3	5.4
WKSS-FM	Pop Contemporary Hit Radio	3.4	4.4	3.4	3.7
WSPR-AM	Spanish Tropical	5.8	2.7	3.3	4.2
WCCC-FM	Active Rock	2.7	3.1	3.0	2.1

This chart shows average quarter hour (AQH) share for listenership among the top ten stations in the Springfield, Massachusetts market area from Fall 2004 through Summer 2005. Audience surveyed was aged 12 and above.

APPENDIX E

▼

SAMPLE RADIO AD COPY

60 sec.—Richardson's Candy Kitchen, Valentine's Day Campaign

If you really find the one you love, there's so much you have in common. In my case, my honey and I love the outdoors, good food, romance and as any other guy ... um ... *(clear throat)* ... great *chocolate!*

I know you were thinking something else but no ... chocolate is the secret love of real men. For me, it's Richardson's unreal dark chocolate pistachio bark, which, by the way, you can't find anywhere else as far as I know.

For my sweetheart, it's Richardsons' triple chocolate truffles, the richest, creamiest, most sinful handmade treats that make my Valentine's Day decision so easy.

What's really cool is that the folks at Richardson's will custom-fill heart-shaped boxes to make just the arrangement you want—or if you're in a hurry there are tons of ready made treats for everyone on your Valentine's Day gift list.

And for something *really* unique and special for your Valentine, try Richardson's hand-dipped chocolate-covered strawberries. These delights are only available on Saturday, Sunday and Monday February 12t thru 14 and must be pre-ordered.

So I guess now you want to know where Richardson's is so you can indulge in your chocolate fantasies? Routes 5 and 10 in South Deerfield, just a few miles up the road from Yankee Candle. Stop by or call them at 772-0443. Richardson's Candy Kitchen.... Believe me, it just doesn't get any better!

APPENDIX F

▼

GLOSSARY OF SELECTED RADIO TERMS

account executive
: A salesperson who sells commercials (air-time) and services clients who buy it

adjacency
: A commercial announcement positioned immediately before or after a specific program or programming segment; e.g., a brokerage firm a might request its spots spot to run "adjacent" to the daily stock reports

affidavit
: A signed statement from a radio station confirming that that an advertiser's commercials were actually run as scheduled; indicates the day and time of each broadcast and accompanies the station's invoice to the advertiser or its agency

air shift
: The length of time that a disk jockey works on the air at a given time; average length is usually four hours (e.g., 6 a.m. to 10 a.m.); typically longer for DJs who do evening and overnight shifts

AM	Refers to "amplitude modulation," a broadcast mode in which the amplitude of a carrier wave varies accordance with some characteristic of the modulating signal; in the U.S., the AM frequency band is 520 kilohertz (kHz) to 1,610 kHz
Arbitron	Research firm involved in nationwide radio audience measurements; Arbitron performs regional surveys and provides data to radio stations and advertisers
availabilities	Inventory of commercial time available for any particular hour, day, week, or program; also called "avails"
average quarter hour	Average number of persons in a demographic group who listen to radio for at least 5 minutes during a 15-minute segment; e.g., "men 18 and older, Monday-Friday, 6 AM-Noon, NYC metro area, Jan/Feb 2007, WCBS = 78,400"; used in Arbitron reports
billboard	An announcement identifying a sponsor at the beginning or end of a program; e.g., "This game is brought to you by ..."
call letters	Letters assigned by the Federal Communications Commission (FCC) to identify broadcast stations, e.g., WCBS or KMOX; in the East, call letters usually begin with a "W"; in the West, with a "K"
call sheet	A tracking system listing a salesperson's projected and actual sales calls, spots sold, etc.; usually administered by sales management

coverage	In radio (and other media) the number of households that can tune in to a station because they are within reach of the station's broadcast signal
copy	The written material, or "script" for a radio commercial
CPM	Cost per thousand; the advertiser's cost for reaching 1,000 listeners
cume	Abbreviation for "cumulative audience"; an estimate of a station's total audience over a particular time period; similar to "circulation" for newspapers
dayparts	A system of segmenting the broadcast day for the scheduling of commercials; e.g., 6 a.m.–10 a.m., 10 a.m.–3 p.m., 3 p.m.–7 p.m., 7 p.m. 12 mid, 12 mid–6 a.m.
drive time	Periods during the morning and evening commutes commuting when the largest radio audience is available and hence, radio advertising is most expensive; morning drive time is usually from 6 a.m. to 10 a.m., and evening drive time from 3 p.m. to 7 p.m.
flight	A period of consecutive days or weeks of advertising within an overall ad campaign; e.g., a 10-day flight, a 3-week flight
FM	A broadcast technology that uses "frequency modulation" (FM) to provide high-fidelity sound over broadcast radio; in the U.S. the FM broadcast band is 87.8 megahertz (MHz) to 108.0 MHz.

frequency	In radio advertising, the number of times the target audience will be exposed to a message; also refers to the broadcast frequency of a station, e.g., 1240 AM; 101.5 FM
grid	Rate cards often used by larger radio stations which list options in advertising rates; fees range in direct proportion to the station's inventory, i.e., during high-demand periods, the grid used displays the highest rates.
liners	Short (usually 10 to 15 seconds) image lines or event mentions read live by announcers
log	The program log, produced by a station's traffic department, which lists the entire schedule of programs and commercials in their assigned times for the broadcast day
make good	Commercial that replaces a previously scheduled commercial that either aired incorrectly or not at all (e.g., if a ball game was cancelled, or a scheduled spot is preempted by breaking news)
overnight	The midnight to 6 a.m. daypart
PSA	Public service announcement; announcement for a non-profit organization or event aired at no charge
spot	Shorthand for "commercial announcement"; e.g., a 3-second "spot"
rate card	A list of the standard rates for a radio/TV station, network, publication, website, or any other advertising medium.

rating	Estimate of audience size represented as a percentage of a total group of people surveyed; usually expressed in terms of households or individuals; e.g., a "Female 18-35 rating of 3.5" for a radio station means that 3.5% of all women 18-35 in a market listen to a certain radio station during an Average Quarter Hour
reach	The number of individuals who will be exposed to an advertiser's message within the limits of a radio station's broadcast signal
remote	a live broadcast from a store, event, concert, usually in cooperation with one or more advertisers
ROS	Run of station (or run of schedule); commercial announcements which can be scheduled at the station's discretion anytime during the period specified by the advertiser; e.g., "ROS 35 spots 6 a.m.–midnight, Monday through Sunday"
share	The number of persons who listened to a station during a given time period, expressed as a percent of all persons who listened to radio during that time period; often confused with "ratings" as both are listed as percentages; note that rating always relates to a total market area population, whereas "share" always is expressed in terms of the total listening/viewing activity taking place during a given time period

SMSA

Standard Metropolitan Statistical Area; a market area determined by the U.S. Census Bureau; each SMSA (or "metro area") features a county or counties having at least one central city with population of 50,000 or more, or a city with at least 25,000 which interacts economically or socially with surrounding communities bringing the total population to 50,000

sweeps

A rating period when audience measurements are taken by a surveying organization, such as Arbitron; stations will often run high-profile promotions during sweeps periods

syndicated program

A program offered by an independent organization for sale to stations or advertisers

talent fee

Fee paid to on-air staff for appearances at station events and live broadcasts; also a fee for doing voiceovers for commercials

TAP

Total Audience Plan; a radio buy in which the advertiser purchases a specified number of spots spread throughout the various dayparts; e.g., 1/3 morning/ evening drive, 1/3, daytime, 1/3 evening/ overnight

About the Authors

Bob Diamond was born in New York City in 1948 and lived and went to school there through the 1960s. He then moved to western Massachusetts and completed his education at the University of Massachusetts and started work as a social worker. In 1981 he became a part-time sports announcer at WHAI AM-FM in Greenfield, Mass. and shortly thereafter made the transition to radio sales, where he has been for more than 30 years. He lives in rural western Mass., and his passions are raising money for charities, cross country skiing, coaching basketball, golf, and good food.

Jay Frost is a freelance writer who has authored several books, live training programs, case studies and multimedia scripts for dozens of well-known national corporations, mostly in the pharmaceutical and biotechnology industries. He is author of *Be Brief, be Bright, Be Gone: Career Essentials for Pharmaceutical and Biotechnology Sales Professionals,* the title that inspired *Selling Air.* Jay also lives in rural western Massachusetts and is an avid skier, hiker, and golfer.

978-0-595-47773-9
0-595-47773-9